50

THE CHEMISTRY OF CHANGE

The Chemistry of Change

Problems, Phases and Strategy

François Dupuy

First published in France as *L'Alchime du changement: Problématique, étapes et mise en oeuvre* by Dunod, Paris, 2001

First published in English 2002 by
PALGRAVE
Houndmills, Basingstoke, Hampshire RG21 6XS and
175 Fifth Avenue, New York, N. Y. 10010
Companies and representatives throughout the world

PALGRAVE is the new global academic imprint of
St. Martin's Press LLC Scholarly and Reference Division and
Palgrave Publishers Ltd (formerly Macmillan Press Ltd).

ISBN 0–333–96837–9

This book is printed on paper suitable for recycling and made from fully managed and sustained forest sources.

A catalogue record for this book is available from the British Library.

Library of Congress Cataloging-in-Publication Data
Dupuy, François.
    The chemistry of change: problems, phases, and strategy/
François Dupuy.
        p.cm.
    Includes bibliographical references and index.
    ISBN 0–333–96837–9 (cloth)
        1. Organizational change. I. Title.
    HD58.8.D87 2001
    658.4'06—dc21   2001032759

10   9   8   7   6   5   4   3   2
11   10   09   08   07   06   05   04   03   02

Printed and bound in Great Britain by
Antony Rowe Ltd, Chippenham, Wiltshire

The steersman who shall undertake, while being drunk, to pilot a vessel, shall be fined one hundred shillings and banned from piloting.

In reality, if this article were followed to the letter, bans would be so frequent and so multiple, that there would almost never be any pilots in work, so much are seafaring men, around the ports, subject to getting themselves drunk. And what is remarkable, is that there are pilots and other watermen who never show so much ability and forethought all at the same time, as when they are drunk to a certain point.

The best is nonetheless not to rely on them, if only because of the difficulty in distinguishing the degree of drunkenness which would not be dangerous. And for this the remedy is simple, since the master is free to refuse any pilot who is recognised to be drunk: if he subsequently allows him to become drunk on board, this will be his fault alone.

Translation of extract from the French
New commentary on Naval regulations, of August 1681
Book IV Title III: Inshore pilots, article 8

Contents

List of Figures

Acknowledgements

The conception and composition of this book owe a great deal to the constant support of the Centre Européen d'Education Permanente (CEDEP). Not only did CEDEP finance part of the research used for writing the book but it also provided an ideal place for the free exchange of ideas and opinions, whether with companies or with faculty. Through its Director-General, Claude Michaud, I would like to thank all those who work in this establishment – they all contribute towards an enquiring and amicable environment.

The Kelley School of Business at Indiana University in Bloomington has regularly welcomed me and given me all the resources needed for working on my research in optimal conditions of material and moral comfort. Its Management and Executive Education departments have encouraged me to pursue my reflections on change and have contributed to the collation of the necessary raw material.

This book (and my *The Customer's Victory*) owes everything to the companies and the administrations discussed and analysed. While some of my judgements may be severe, I look upon such organisations with much sympathy.

Last, but not least, Dominique Thomas – always with the same patience, the same competence and the same confidence – has continued in her role of advising, encouraging, reading and correcting. One needs a great deal of abnegation to do all this simultaneously, and yet she has never made an issue of it!

FRANÇOIS DUPUY

Introduction

Change is a recurrent topic in management literature. It is present in all books and articles, and at the same time has become almost an obsession, not only for managers but also all those who, today, work in our organisations, whether in the public or private sector. Even political leaders known to be conservatives or would-be progressives, define themselves in relation to it: being against change, whatever the sphere under consideration, is held to be backward, 'out of touch' and, to say it all, blinkered.

This trend reveals a phenomenon that is at the same time simple and universally accepted, or at least in developed countries – change exists. This is an undisputable fact and there is little point in spending too much time and effort on expounding it. Even if, of course, we do not yet have sufficient hindsight fully to assess the importance and true reach of events that are taking place under our eyes, we can still feel, even at the reduced scale of our own lives, that we shall not end this life in the world in which we started. There are many books that give sophisticated demonstrations and analyses of the spiralling transformation of all aspects of our daily life and the world in which we live.

As far as organisations are concerned – and they are after all the subject of this book – we are now seeing an interesting paradox, which certainly merits some attention: it is not so much change itself that poses a problem. It is even valued as a driving force for economic activity, as a source for the creation of wealth; it is the ability to lead it, to steer it, to control it, in brief to be an 'active actor' and not just a simple spectator, even if enthusiastic. Steering change has become one of today's major issues for managers – for reasons that are easy to understand and that have little to do with the megalomania which is supposed to have blossomed in Orwell's footsteps.

WHY THE COST OF UNCONTROLLED CHANGE HAS BECOME INTOLERABLE

In the conventional industrial world, where we have mass production, Taylorism, Fordism or triumphant administration, in this world where one used to ask for goods and services even before asking for the bill, the extra costs of uncontrolled change never appeared to be intolerable since they never appeared at all. The accounting systems themselves did not disclose them and they just ended up buried under 'progress', a concept that was general enough to absorb, without too much difficulty, errors that were not necessarily insignificant.

Today, the picture is different. Everything is calculated, everything is measured, everything is assessed: we don't look solely at defects, but also at the costs of non quality. In more general terms, such measurement focuses as much on what is not as on what is and the accounting systems mentioned above have adapted to this. The result, not only for managers but also for all those with responsibility at any level whatsoever, is a twofold require-ment: first, change is necessary because it is a condition for survival, but also it is necessary at a controlled cost and, where possible, a reduced cost, and hence it is necessary to control the movement.

Let us say this right away, some people do not stop to consider that this is an impossible task and that it would be better not to attempt it. Books and articles make their appearance regularly, written by reputed authors who emphasise that 'change programmes don't produce change',[1] who wonder 'why transformation efforts fail',[2] or who state, even more directly and unambiguously, that one does not 'manage change'.[3] And the fact is that, despite all the attempts to predict everything, master everything, control everything, this just does not happen. The phenomenon remains largely unpredictable, produces unexpected effects and leaves those respon-sible, those in charge, to a great extent perplexed if not in a total quandary. It is true that, as Peter Drucker says,[4] our organisations are designed more for stability than for change, rather in the same way that our managers have been trained more to ensure continuity than to manage or introduce disruption.

As a result, there is a real obsession with the 'action plan', through which one attempts to predict everything, organise everything, control everything right down to the smallest detail, and the establishment of which becomes an essential condition for 'launching oneself' and, at the same time, an end in itself. This way of looking at things of course leads to a form of paralysis since nothing can be completely predicted or planned. The actual commencement of the process itself always finds itself pushed back until, through necessity, that is, external constraints becoming ever more pressing, one no longer has a choice, one is backed against the wall, or, to put it more brutally, in a crisis situation. But change through crisis, so well described and analysed, and for so long, by Michel Crozier[5] is even more painful in human terms and, in general, even more costly. It therefore no longer corresponds to the needs of the moment, and only organisations which are not yet entirely under constraints of accountability – public authorities for example[6] – can allow themselves this privilege.

SEEKING REASSURANCE OR TRYING TO CONTROL EVENTS?

Of course, when faced with the random element of any action for change, such hesitation brings a smile to the faces of all those 'intermediaries of change', people whose work is rather like that of paediatricians – reassuring anxious mothers even before treating their children, in other words, reassuring managers before doing anything at all. This is what creates business for consultancy firms, and one can understand that the more urgent the need is for change, the more their market expands and the more their involvement increases. After all, the primary function of such involvement is to legitimise what has been done, to release the manager from all or part of his responsibility, which finally has no price. At the same time, it is important to acknowledge that resorting to such intermediation is a first step indicating that there is an awareness of the need to make things evolve. The temptation remains to do nothing, to protect oneself, to wait for the storm to pass, and to cover up such immobility with an impressive smokescreen of sophisticated action plans, skilfully prioritised projects, focus groups, surveys and work. In brief, substituting agitation for action, until the process itself becomes paralysed and loses itself in uncontrollable meanderings about which, after a while, nobody worries any more. The major European transport company which, in a way, will serve as the guiding thread for this book, is a living example of this: confronted with increasingly vigorous intermodal competition, but at the same time prisoner of an impressive conservatism finally shared by its managers as much as by the union organisations, it initiated over 50 'priority action programmes' which, put end to end, form its 'business project', tie up considerable energies, time, money and so on – only to produce at the end of the day an evident immobility and this to the great satisfaction of all protagonists: it's so hard to do nothing while moving about so much!

So, one might say, what is the point of another work on this non-event known as change? Why add another stone to this edifice – so hopeless or so well constructed, depending on the angle from which it is viewed? Can such a book aim for a result other than simultaneously to provide food for ambient discussions and conservatism? Certainly, for when one looks closely, one finds a few experiences of successful change: one of their characteristics is that those who conducted them did not seek to control everything nor indeed manage everything, but instead accepted uncertainty and, finally, did not consider it absolutely essential to know their destination in order to get there. Maybe they had no choice. But so much the worse or so much the better: there is something to be learned and adopted from their approaches. One can start with something that they themselves point out – thus joining the ranks of some of the authors referred to above.[7] They have wagered on knowledge – that is, they did not want to hide from reality – at the same time as on trust – they wanted to share such knowledge with those who were most concerned by change: their workforce.

THE IMPORTANCE OF KNOWLEDGE AND KNOWLEDGE SHARING

In saying that, one cannot help thinking of Air France between 1993 and 1998, and the famous 'method' which took its name from their CEO of that time. We will be using this case a great deal in this book. And one cannot help being struck by how nonconformist and unusual this approach appears in relation to our ways of thinking, our education and our habits. Confronting reality, seeing it as it really is and not just as one would like it to be, in other words *listening*, is disturbing for managers, who are there because they are supposed to know more than others about how things are, how they must be, and how to achieve this. Such acceptance of reality shows modesty but also boldness, both of which have to be learned, as suggested by Chris Argyris.[8]

However, as shown previously,[9] such access to knowledge cannot be spontaneous, unless by exception which is all the more remarkable for being an exception. To be successful, this requires time – but not haste, agitation or hyperactivity. It needs true intellectual investment, which presupposes learning and mastering new ways of reasoning, usually very different from those taught to our elites, whichever schools or universities they attend, or on whichever side of the Atlantic they find themselves. In particular, it requires their agreement to do without the models – quantitative, organisational, behavioural, etc – that give reassurance but also block the view and impede listening. It is not at all surprising that each of us seeks to connect the part of reality that confronts us to a vaster whole that is already known. In a stressful situation, like those that demand the implementation of change, this reduces uncertainty and allows the use of solutions that have been 'tried and tested' in circumstances that appear to be similar. But there is a substantial risk of not really trying to get to grips with the specific reality with which one is confronted. Experience teaches us that we must listen, it does not tell us what we must hear.

Sharing knowledge – we will return to this more fully – is an even more unusual experience, since it presupposes *trust*, an approach which is as unfamiliar to our organisations as investment in knowledge. Since the industrial world became the industrial world, that is, when work was no

longer described by poets but analysed and organised by specialists, efforts
have been immense and continual towards reducing the inherent uncertainty
in human behaviour. From rules to organisation charts, from recommendations to procedures, everything is done to make what people do at work predictable and above all independent of their good intentions or, even worse,
their arbitrary nature. Basically, never more than in business have people
been judged as so fundamentally bad and unworthy of trust. Hence all the
rhetoric on 'resistance to change' which so marked the 1970s and 1980s and
which served as a windbreak to the immobility of a good number of managers. People – but who are these 'people'? – would not like change and so
it is necessary to impose it on them and to watch carefully that they do
exactly what they are supposed to do. It is not particularly important that
they know why they are being asked to change: they are just expected to
apply the new instructions, to come, to go, to follow, and then everything
will be all right.

One only needs to watch one's children to see that military logic, which
Robert Reich[10] noted had durably marked our companies since the end of
World War II, no longer works. If one understands that an organisation is
first and foremost a structure of human behaviours – of rational strategies
as we might say in this book – then one can understand that actors will
only agree to modify these behaviours if one shares with them the necessity for change, that is, the final problem that one is seeking to resolve.
This is what we mean here by the sharing of knowledge, which puts everybody on the same level and which, no doubt, leaves the king naked but
restores a certain independence and margin for manoeuvre to his subjects.

However, while it is true that one cannot control everything, plan everything nor indeed organise everything, it is possible to propose an approach
that, while modest, makes it possible to tackle the problems outlined
above, those of knowledge and trust. This approach is centred on organisations, for, as we have already discussed in a previous book,[11] it is they who
are concerned, first and foremost, with change: under pressure from customers, they need to reappraise, often urgently, their normal 'ways of functioning', that is the way in which their members work, make decisions,
resolve their problems, cooperate or, to the contrary, defend themselves.

USING STRATEGIC ANALYSIS OF ORGANISATIONS

The frame of reference will be that of the strategic analysis of organisations, although its use will be extended, in view of the latest experiences of
leading change associated with this mode of reasoning. In fact, until
recently, organisational analysis has primarily been used as a knowledge

tool, of which the relevance today is no longer contested by anybody. It is now important to take another step forward and, in the light of new case studies, see what this same tool can contribute in the phases following the initial diagnosis. This, as we will see, retains all its importance since it allows us to highlight the *problems* that an action of change is supposed to handle. However, because the basic postulate of organisational analysis is that of *bounded rationality*[12] – of the intelligence of actors – this makes it possible to continue and to work on terms and conditions which favour the behavioural evolution of such intelligent actors. One should not underestimate to what extent this idea of intelligence, when one has a thorough understanding of all its implications, can be demanding and off-putting compared with conventional management approaches – marked by suspicion, doubt and the necessity for control in the narrowest sense of the term. At the same time, it is easy to anticipate that this is what establishes the foundation and legitimacy of the transition through *trust*.

This transition is made necessary by the increase in independence, information, capacity for choice and therefore intelligence of those working in our organisations. All are not yet *knowledge workers*,[13] although the tendency is moving in that direction. We are thus confronted with populations who are more inclined to question the orders given to them, to be more critical if what is proposed does not correspond to an apprehension based on reality – their reality.

The positive aspect of this new requirement lies in the opportunities that it provides. Starting from reality, therefore from knowledge, is a necessity that is even less contestable in that it is so necessary to reduce the human and financial costs of change. But once this investment is made, it can be valorised by associating all parties with such knowledge, and involving them in the search for practical solutions that focus on their own behaviours, and not simply on structures, or on attitudes.

PROBLEMATICS, SEQUENCING AND IMPLEMENTATION OF CHANGE

Three angles of approach to change can thus be seen and will be developed over the following pages:

1. The first focuses on the *problematics of change*. What needs to be modified, developed, transformed when talking of change?

   Does one simply want to correct *attitudes*, – the way in which people express themselves, the references that they use, even their vocabulary? One would then be looking at a simple transformation of *culture*, in the most usual sense of the term, the one most freely used in companies and which is assimilated to a vague structure of behavioural norms with no true impact on real behaviour.[14]

Is it more a question of modifying structures, organisation charts, rules and procedures, that is, all that encompasses the action? But one then returns to the simplistic idea that the actors do what is effectively written into instructions and therefore that good rules make good organisations. However, we have known for a long time that, while rules structure the game, they do not delineate it. They are an essential element and strategic reasoning will help to understand how they can be used to leverage change and why they cannot be used to lead it.

More fundamentally, returning to a sociological definition of organisations, which appears to be the most relevant and operational option, it will be shown that the main challenge is to act on the strategies of actors, that is, on the solutions that they find, in the context in which they have been put, in order to resolve the problems that they are trying to resolve. It is then easy to understand that this problematic of change does not make things easy and leaves little room for the usual strategies of protection. It is in fact even more difficult to act in a relevant and reasoned manner on strategies developed by intelligent actors, than to proceed with a simple reorganisation of structures which, most of the time, is only a concern for bosses or apparatchiks who want to conserve their territories. *A fortiori*, changing behaviours – the strategies – is a more perilous undertaking than modifying the attitudes which are, in general, only the resultant.

2. What has been discussed above suggests a *sequencing* of change – not a rigid and tightly controlled schedule, but rather a framework for action, phases inside which structures can be built.

The first of these phases will not be surprising if one considers what has been said above: it consists of moving on from *symptoms* to *problems*. What starts an action of change is most often an 'alert', a signal that lights up and indicates that something is not right. The pressure for continuity is so great, in our organisations, that change is primarily a reaction, a defence mechanism, arising when the threat is seen as sufficiently serious. It is rarely a case of anticipation, although when this is the case, the instigator of the action, however highly placed in the hierarchy, is seen as seriously lacking in legitimacy.

But what is apparent in the first place – worsening results, loss of market share, increasing numbers of defects, breakdowns, delays, abnormal absenteeism – is the presence of symptoms in the proper sense of the term. These indicate a problem, but do not actually say what that problem is. It is here that investment in knowledge takes on its full meaning and that strategic reasoning shows its full acuity, making it possible to go right up to the problems, that is, right up to the *organisa-tional mechanisms* that will enable interpretation of the initial symptoms. This movement is a crucial phase in any process of change: it avoids unnecessary conflict arising around unofficial interpretations proposed by the different actors, at the same time as absolving them from blame by means of the systemic interpretation that it offers. It breaks the tacit and often punitive agreement between managers and consultants to move on directly from symptoms to solutions, a sort of consensus based on misunderstanding. Finally, it avoids wasting energy pointlessly trying to find solutions to problems of which one is not aware.

Once the real subjects that must be tackled have been identified, a twofold difficulty then appears:

- the first aspect lies in the multitude of sites that must be opened if one wants to cover the whole area revealed. This is part of a logic that has already been discussed, that of overall comprehensiveness which, as we have emphasised, has both a paralysing and dilutive effect on action;
- the second is linked to the *billiard ball* effect which is a consequence induced by systemic analysis: by reconstituting the overall logic, that is, the prioritisation of parties in relation to one another and in relation to the whole, systemic analysis produces a picture of coherence which is pleasing intellectually but useless in practical terms, as it allows little or no identification of the cracks and ledges onto which one can cling in order to start climbing up the cliff-face of change.

Getting away from these two apparent dead-ends presupposes the definition of *priorities* which correspond, not to subjects identified as the most serious or the most urgent, but to the points by which the system under consideration may start to lose its equilibrium. In this area, a few practical suggestions can be made, which once again rely on strategic reasoning: these make it possible to show how, with analysis, the identification of the principal resource of the most powerful actor is a worthwhile path leading to the nodal point of operation for the system under consideration. This is what sociologists have sometimes called the *regulation* of this system, and it is this which most often needs to be changed.

But not by decree. Not by a linear reasoning that ordains that when the priority has been identified as A, it is on A that action must be focused. This needs to be thought out in terms of *levers* – points, places in the organisation on which one can act, which perhaps do not appear to be central, but which help to develop the strategies of actors, and therefore change the real methods of functioning.

3. There remains the *implementation*. This is certainly the main stumbling block in any process of change, no matter how this has been designed. At the end of the day, the main difficulty does not consist of developing brilliant ideas or huge programmes bearing the hallmark of commonsense found in formal logic: rather, it consists of implementing them. There has already been much discussion on the need for experimentation before generalising or, to the contrary, changing the 'predominant reference system' in an organisation fundamentally and in a single move. Similarly, earlier writers have heavily emphasised the necessary 'caution' as soon as it involves changing working habits or modifying the territories of various people. And no doubt it is true that, in its implementation phase, change is an eminently political process, as in the Athenian sense of city administration.

But if we return to the idea of trust, then it is possible to think that actors in an organisation must also be actors of change. This involves an *opportunity*, or a moment in the organisation's life which makes it legitimate to refer to its members and capture their interest, in both senses of the term. The symptom mentioned above can play this role to the extent that it is difficult to start change from cold, even if, intellectually, this would be more satisfying. Finally, and whatever they say about it, organisations rarely have other strategies in preparing for the future than to consolidate the past. However, such a symptom, mostly experienced as a drama, a catastrophe, a constraint, can be used as a *resource*. This is what is generally known as opportunity management and it is, at the end of the day, a question of timing in seizing bodily upon the issue even before the signal warning of danger finally announces the catastrophe.

The trust to which we refer, not because of a humanist predisposition but through the evidence of experience, is what makes it possible to motivate energies in the *understanding* of problems, the search for solutions and their *acceptance*, when they have acquired a collective and not partisan legitimacy.

We should point out finally that this book has been structured on the basis of real-life case studies, on which we have had the opportunity to work over recent years. They are therefore used here on the understanding that their presentation does not cause problems for the organisations concerned. As a precautionary measure, most of them have been rendered anonymous. This is the guarantee that only the reality – of which we will be seeking knowledge throughout this book – will be taken into account. Indeed, we will see that reviewing reality by means of knowledge tools, makes it possible to play down its importance sufficiently to make it a purpose for action and not a subject for biased arguments.

1 Change: Yes, But What?

Our organisations need to undergo a profound and continual process of change if they want to adapt to a world which has revolutionised them in the past and will continue to do so in the future. Every day, management literature produces an impressive catalogue of 'new organisations', new structures, new concepts that illustrate the variety of initiatives introduced virtually across the board in order to face up to the multitude of challenges. Even companies in the 'new economy' have not been able to escape this movement – between 1999 and 2000, eBay, Amazon.com and AOL were all to announce fundamental restructuring programmes, intended to adapt their organisations to a market that was undergoing profound change. From 'communities of practice' to cooperation, presented as the key factor in reducing costs and continually improving quality, not a day goes past without the appearance, on the marketplace for ideas and practices, of some new suggestion in terms of organisation. Such consensus and such proliferation help to explain both the pressures placed on organisations and the hesitations in the responses that are made. There is no longer, as in the good old days of mass production or even, more recently, of triumphant Toyotism, a dominant model that can assert itself and provide a key that guarantees performance under optimal conditions.

In fact, there is no longer any model at all that really focuses on the nature of the organisations that need to be set up, or on their structures and on how to steer them. At present, caution and good sense seem to have won the day by giving priority to the methodologies of steering change rather than to the substance which predefines what must exist.[1] This position, although at first glance less reassuring for managers, is nonetheless far more realistic. It formally acknowledges the fact that organisations are now infinitely more varied than in the past, because they are no longer in a position to impose methods of operation on their markets, allowing them then to resolve their own problems, whether technical or human, rather than resolving those of their customers. They can no longer impose uniformity on an environment which now insists on individuality. The response to this individuality is even more difficult to provide because the world itself has become more complex, the number of 'individualities' to be taken into consideration has never stopped rising alongside the simultaneous appearance of increasing numbers of contradictions between the end results that are needed in order to satisfy everybody.

1

Even 'best practices', so popular because they make it possible to learn from the experience of others, have become more methodological rather than substantive: in an article published by the *Harvard Business Review*, Jerry Stermin and Robert Choo[2] show how, in terms of change, companies could benefit enormously from the experience of non-profit organisations. Analysing what they call 'the power of positive deviancy', they tell the story of an association working to reduce malnutrition in Vietnamese children: having seen that the children of one village community seemed better fed and more healthy, they tried to find out why. They quickly realised that this community had different behaviour patterns, with regard to both what they ate and how often they ate. They therefore tried, with some success, to extend these deviant practices to the surrounding villages. However, they concluded that it was not the types of food – eating more or less fish or greens – that formed the basis of the problem, but the reasoning; that is, the demonstration that it was possible to do things differently from those tradition seemed to have established. In modern business language, we might call that experimentation.

A THEORETICAL DEBATE: TO CENTRALISE OR TO DECENTRALISE?

Organisations are all in the same situation, whether public or private. They are desperately trying to find out what is best, most of the time in terms of structures, and yet are unwilling to invest in methodology – which can indeed be more demanding but so much more rewarding. This is how it has been for years – and still is today – in the theoretical debate on the choice between centralisation and decentralisation. This debate has marked the industrial world for many long years, often in Manichean terms, opposing the two alternatives in a way that makes it obligatory to choose either one or the other, under pain of being accused of incoherence or muddled thinking.[3]

And yet .... A big European industrial glassmaking group – we are talking here about flat glass – has eight factories handling production based on a strictly identical formal organisation; a prime example of the irresistible search for coherence which has just been mentioned. Under the apparent authority – or leadership, we might say today – of the Factory Manager, three deputy managers share out the day-to-day tasks: the technical manager looks after everything relating to the factory's core activity, production and maintenance, which he controls so jealously that even the factory manager himself thinks twice about going round the workshops;

the administrative and financial manager oversees compliance with the management rules in force within the group, which he is expected to see applied in a manner that is strictly identical for all production units; and finally the manager in charge of human relations manages labour relations, within the scope of a national collective agreement and a company agreement covering day-to-day administration – agreements which were negotiated at branch level for the first and at group level for the second, without the factories having been particularly involved in these negotiations between partners who already knew each other well and didn't have to spell things out for each other.

In this context, it is clear that it is the technical manager who really holds the reins of power.[4] He is the one with exclusive control over what is the factory's reason for being, over how it is evaluated and therefore over the conditions for its survival. And even more so because this example is seen at a time when, faced with the group's need to adapt its technical resources, head office still has the prerogative of privileging sites which it considers to be the most cost-effective. Like all actors, the technical manager uses this power with a view to career management which, after all, is the driving force for any organisation: in order to achieve what he wants – carrying out production under optimal conditions while ensuring the full development of industrial equipment – he needs to 'buy' all his teams or, in other words, obtain for them dispensations from the group's rigid rules, whether in terms of promotion, grading or remuneration. In order to reach his goals, he applies constant pressure on his colleagues whom he considers more as subordinates than equals. Meanwhile, they have no intention of allowing themselves to be 'manipulated' in such a way, and so, although they understand what is going on, they hide behind central procedures, thus making things ever more complicated, ever more difficult to achieve and negotiate – an autonomy which the technical manager is always seeking to put through as profit or loss. In brief, this is a classic example of the 'bureaucratic vicious circle' that we are able to observe.

Systemic reasoning enables us to understand the consequences of this game, ultimately without any great surprises, at the level of the flat glass division itself: central management 'functional staff' feed on these local conflicts which help to legitimise their action, and find that their correspondents 'on the spot' are partners who are always looking for more of these rules and procedures which protect them from the absolute power of technical logic. Put briefly, each level reinforces the next without anybody, throughout the progress of each particular decision, anticipating the overall effect of all the micro decisions.

Added to this is an inflationist drift, linked to the dissociation between *real power* and *formal power*. The Factory Manager's position of extreme weakness leads him to seek compensations elsewhere than in the effective management of a unit from which, to all intents and purposes, he is excluded. In order to legitimise his role, he has virtually no other means than always to be asking central financial management for more investments, more financial resources, which will allow him to demonstrate that he is capable of playing a positive and active role in the day-to-day running of the factory. However, there are eight factories in this division, which means eight managers all developing the same strategy of asking for additional financial resources.

We should note here that this is a constant in the life of organisations: *when a line manager lacks the organisational resources to be a relevant actor in the universe that he is supposed to be directing, he always asks for more physical resources, whether in financial or human terms.* This is why the dissociation mentioned above, between real power and formal power, poses a problem that is not aesthetic or moral, but entirely practical: it leads to an ever growing need for resources – not for objective reasons of real needs, but for reasons that can only be qualified as systemic.

In the case under consideration, it is thus the eight factory managers who are placed in the same situation and thus develop the strategy of 'always more'. To get what they need so as not to disappear completely from the game, they manipulate the information that they transmit in support of their various and varied requirements. But the actors in charge of allocating resources have finally understood the game. Incapable of, or perhaps unconcerned about, carrying out the necessary corrections and arbitrations themselves, they allocate resources in line with a bureaucratic logic that enables them to minimise their own risks. Consequently, more has been spent without the resources allocated being suited to real situations and without anybody being really satisfied.

The organisation 'consumes' huge quantities of resources without in fact seeing an increase in its efficiency. This simple observation helps to anticipate to what extent it is a change in the methods of functioning; that is, the way in which the actors 'play', which will become the crucial factor in the process of transformation.

Many will see themselves in the above presentation: there's nothing original about this example. However, incidentally, it helps people to understand some of the very real mechanisms behind the non-control of costs that management accounting tools do not always allow them to grasp. But going beyond this observation, if one investigates possible solutions, one might well reach the conclusion that this universe needs centralisation *as well as* decentralisation: centralisation, because breaking out of the inflationist vicious circle discussed earlier would presuppose transferring control over the factory's 'core activity', in this case responsibility for servicing and maintenance; but decentralisation as well because, while central departments are padded out to such an extent, they will always need to produce more standards and to find allies who will use them as resources in their local strategies.

Here are two useful and amusing anecdotes to illustrate the above: when the technical manager at the biggest factory was himself made Factory Manager, he immediately requested, and was granted, that the job of technical manager be abolished in his new unit. In the same way, when the results of this diagnostic work were shown to the group's Chief Executive Officer, he showed himself to be dubious about the need for drastically reducing staff levels in the central Human Resources Department – until the day when he saw, under the windows of his own office, situated in a well-to-do suburb in the capital, twenty or so workers from a factory located somewhere far away in the distant provinces fiercely demanding an increase in their job grading coefficient, for the reason that the person in charge of such questions in the factory had led them to understand that such a decision could only be made at the highest level. You might call this active learning.

It is *not*, therefore, mainly through the use of substantive models, which are nonetheless very popular among managers and directors, that one can manage the problem of change. In any case, it is common knowledge that most of them have already fallen by the wayside, although this does not seem to stop people from suggesting new ones. Their therapeutic value, which comes close to how paediatricians describe their role – that of reassuring mothers – cannot be denied. But that is not enough on its own to legitimise their exclusive use on a daily basis. We will therefore be forced to turn towards *methodology*, that is, reasoning, and accept that progress will be slow and sometimes hesitant, without the hope of covering all aspects of a process of change, and without the possibility of escaping from all those lucky or not so lucky surprises that this process is certain to hold.

CHANGE BY ACTING ON STRUCTURES

Perhaps, first of all, we should avoid putting the cart before the horse and try to reach agreement *on what needs to be changed*, once we decide our organisation must evolve. With regard to this aspect, the first temptation has always been, implicitly or explicitly, to give an answer in terms of structures, and to see the driving force of change in the modification of organisation charts, in the re-arrangement of responsibilities, in the amendment of rules and procedures. Many debates have nurtured this vision of things, if only those focusing on the advantages and disadvantages of 'flat structures' as opposed to more hierarchical structures, on the merits and drawbacks of 'matrix structures' and so on. These cause directors and the consultants that they hire to redefine continually the 'processes', the job descriptions, the organisation charts – based on the belief that all these things will in fact correspond to the reality. And yet, when one looks closely, there is a curious paradox hidden behind this way of doing things.

The realisation that organisation does not equate with structure is not so very recent.[5] It is based on the frequently observed fact that organisations do not function in accordance with their official definitions, nor indeed with the rules and procedures, so long and carefully weighed up, which are assumed to define their boundaries. This truth asserts itself to the point that, in current language, we talk of a *zeal strike* where a given category of staff decides to work to rule and apply absolutely all the regulations that it is supposed to apply. Now, as none of these categories is permanently on strike, it is easy to conclude that the application of official standards is an exception – and not the rule. Similarly, one might conclude that this abundance or even, *a fortiori*, overabundance of procedures, makes organisations even less predictable even though its purpose is to instil clarity and transparency. This is what one might call the 'paradox of regulations'[6] which, in the most bureaucratic organisations, produces reversed hierarchies; that is, situations in which the managers manifestly depend more upon subordinates than subordinates upon managers, to the extent that the inapplicability of rules forces the latter to call increasingly upon the goodwill of the former – who themselves expect ever more regulations, on the one hand, to cover themselves and, on the other, to increase their own freedom.

This assimilation of the organisation to the structure also leads to an entirely static and abstract vision of power according to which power is seen as the equivalent of the official hierarchy. Outside any theoretical discussion – and there is more than enough of that – if this were true, it would become very difficult to explain why, in so many organisations, when one wants to get rid of a troublesome actor, this actor is given a promotion and, what is more, is usually under no illusion as to the meaning of the reward that he has just received.

But there is more, and this is even more serious. The distinction between organisation and structure has direct consequences on the *strategy* of change.

In particular, it legitimises the preference for a participative approach, which will be the case throughout this book. For, if an organisation were able to reduce itself to its corpus of rules and written standards, then changing it could be effected by injunction, based on an extensive use of consultants commissioned to redefine and redesign the new entity, after a rapid analysis. If, to the contrary, one understands that there is a great deal more to change and that one must look towards real behaviours – or strategies, as we will come to say – then one must rely far more on trust, on the development of capabilities, on the inventiveness of all those involved.[7]

Paradoxically, this idea is relatively well accepted intellectually but little used in practice. A big company, world leader in its market, came to see us with the following question: over the previous year, with help from a large and well-known consulting firm, it had redefined a new structure that was better suited to the perception that it had of its market. The past twelve months had been devoted to setting out the new principles in terms of management rules, accounting rules, reporting rules, human resources rules and so on. Our contacts told us that this now involved putting in place the methods of functioning; that is, the actual way in which actors would use what had just been developed at huge expense. In brief, it was now necessary, finally, to look closely at the organisation, and those responsible were well aware that this would not only be more difficult than the preceding phase and in quite different ways but, even more importantly, could not be conducted in the same manner. Already, the troops were grumbling against the ambient *authoritarianism*, and pressure was mounting more and more strongly for everybody to be called on to participate in the next phase – the only one that really counted in the eyes of all those concerned.

What has just been recounted through this example appears to be a matter of common sense, especially as, when told like this, in simple terms, it wins everybody's support. And yet the consequences in terms of change are only rarely deduced, and companies continue to prefer approaches focusing on structures, once they have accepted the need to modify their organisation. In so doing, they have control over neither the *process* that they have implemented, nor the *results* that they achieve, thus increasing the unwillingness of managers to take action, as well as the phenomenon of resistance from those who, rightly or wrongly, feel that their territory is under threat. An outside observer is sure to be fascinated by the amount of time, energy and, of course, money expended in this way on laboriously defining the 'new structures', new processes, new rules – and all this for results that are inadequate if not diametrically opposed to those that were officially expected. Surprisingly, this can open up room for action: a manager's biggest worry, when he has just exhausted his political talents in implementing an organisation chart acceptable to everybody, is that he will be expected to rework it. In a confidential manner, his colleagues let him know that that they can take 'anything, but not that'. Which means that everything is possible! More, even – it also signifies great freedom for working on the day-to-day reality provided the end results are acceptable. Sometimes directors themselves call for this work that they vaguely feel the need for.

This is what happened in a major North American company in the food-processing sector. In order to cope with expansion and diversification, it needed to develop rapidly one of its factories, until then in single production, towards a capacity for rapid changeover of brands or products in line with market requirements. To this was added the necessity for a fast improvement in quality together with the eradication of delays in terms of product availability. That was a lot to ask. A new factory manager was appointed and the project for change was put in his hands. Seconded to him were a number of young, high quality and ambitious managers, with whom he formed his executive committee. These young managers, looking on their stay in this factory as only a minor step in their career paths, represented the group's functional management divisions on the site, such as the Industrial Division, all of which were big producers of regulations and procedures intended to harmonise the overall procedures for doing things in all of the group's factories. Nothing worked as planned. The executive committee never managed to reach an integrated vision, and each member took refuge in his own particular logic without worrying about the rest. As a result, procedures were seen as too complex, obscure and contradictory, piling up one on top of another. Payroll costs rose because of the need for new recruits to manage the increasingly complicated dealings with the rest of the group. At the end of day, the manager was given to understand that his true job consisted of bending the rules and that it was his ability to adapt that would be evaluated as a priority. It was from that moment on that he was able to get to work seriously and instigate the necessary changes.

THE DECLARATION OF GOOD TAX CONDUCT

Here is another example of the mechanisms that we have described above which, in this particular case, takes place in the public sector and shows that nobody has a monopoly on blindly following rules. In a particular large European tax administration office there is a conventional – although not legally defined – distinction between the 'certifying officer', who calculates the amount of tax payable, and the 'accountant' who deals with its collection, even if such separation suffers from a certain number of exceptions depending on the type of taxation. The result of this, of course, is a huge complexity for the taxpayer, who, even if sometimes able to use the situation to advantage, is generally shunted from one department to another, from one person to another and watches, powerlessly, over the improbable routing of his increasingly 'virtual' file. Of course, the people in charge of this administration are not unaware of such difficulties and, under the pressure of public opinion, conveyed by the spur of political power, it was decided to try out the idea of a 'single tax representative' who will be available, in a single location, to respond to questions and requests from taxpayers. This happy initiative was tried out on a single specific case – delivery of the 'declaration of good tax conduct'.

Under this fancy name is hidden a simple mechanism – that of the usual technical bureaucracies – which can be described as follows: when an individual or a business decides to take part in a public invitation to tender, they must demonstrate that they are in order with regard to their payment of taxes and social security contributions. The intention is certainly praiseworthy, and it meets a need from businesses themselves that would like to be able prevent competitors from being able to put in lower bids than them through not paying their various liabilities to the State and social security bodies.

There are three different documents that are needed: the first stating that one has properly paid one's taxes, obtained from the Inland Revenue; the second certifying that one has paid one's value added tax, delivered by the local Treasury Office; and the third confirming that one is up-to-date with filing one's tax declarations, obtained from the Tax Office. It is easy to see all the difficulty and time involved in such procedures. This was why a ministerial circular ruled that, as of a given date, it was the paymaster who would deliver this precious document, with the responsibility of obtaining the necessary papers from colleagues in other departments concerned and within the required time limit for responding to the invitation to tender.

The result is easy to picture: it rapidly became apparent that delivery of the notorious declaration was proving extremely difficult, if not actually impossible in certain cases, causing the unfortunate paymaster in charge of delivering it to provide whoever applied for it with a 'default declaration', which in fact states the *organisational* impossibility of delivering the document in question, a declaration which is even more useless in that it does not authorise participation in the invitation to tender, even when this is issued by one of the bodies which has contributed to the above-mentioned default. This situation might well be qualified as grotesque.

Why such a stalemate in what was indeed an attempt at change focusing on a real problem that arises frequently for the customer/taxpayer? Are those who made the decision unaware and are those who applied it irresponsible? Certainly neither one nor the other. Quite simply, each side believed that what was written into the rule would actually happen, and that action is produced by the text that defines it. This is a vision of action which can be described as bureaucratic or linear, as opposed to a strategic and systemic vision which we will define later and which is often very far-removed from how managers reason, whether in the public or the private sector.

In reality, things turned out rather like this. Between the different organisations involved, there exist traditional rivalries which we will not be expanding on here, but which result in each side watching jealously over their autonomy and, if given the opportunity, with no hesitation in complicating the other side's task in order to convey their situation of dependency. To this can be added the jealousies linked to differences in official or non-official remunerations. The paymaster, in the system that has just been described, arouses a certain amount of animosity because the others, rightly or wrongly, feel that he is in a privileged position. From the moment that he is asked to be the sole point of contact for the requester, *in a situation where he is dependant on others in order to reply to the request*, these others will not be prepared to put the necessary enthusiasm and speed into the task. Even worse, and here the example invites reflection on the unexpected effects of uncontrolled action, from the bidding company's point of view, one finds a situation far worse than the one that was hopefully being remedied: in the earlier situation, however painful the procedures might be, the requester still retained a certain level of control over the process. He could go to the offices, pressurise or even plead. In this new situation, not only is it more difficult to obtain the necessary papers but the requester cannot even have access to those who deliver them. His degree of control over the situation is singularly affected and finally the *quality* of the service provided has deteriorated. This mechanism does not affect only the system that has just been described.[8]

What is really at stake, therefore, is not the 'right rules', those saying how things *ought* to be. We should always bear in mind that, when talking of action, the conditional tense has only negative virtues. It is used more for self-protection than for getting things moving. This does not imply that rules are pointless – after all, what is an organisation without rules? – or that they cannot be used as *levers*, but rather that one must get away from visions that are mechanistic, simplistic and blinkered. And the same can be said for the 'right structures', those defining where each person should be and what they should be doing. This approach to change, likening it to a game of Meccano, ends up in the same dead-ends, one might almost say the same lottery, so random is the final result with so much remaining to be done for whoever wants to control it.

FORMAL ORGANISATION AND REAL ORGANISATION

Michael Hammer and Steven Stanton give a very illustrative example of this observation in analysing the reasons for failure in the transition from a conventional organisation to a process organisation. They observe that this change was conducted, at least to start with, by 'redesigning' the company's structures, and that this strategy resulted in a dead-end to the extent, as they put it, that, even when the design was good, the real organisation was opposed to it. They observe that 'the problem was not in the design of the process. The problem was that power continued to lie in the old functional departments'.[9] The simple fact of distinguishing, as do these authors, between *organisation* and *real organisation* tells us more than all those sophisticated theories on the extraordinary abstraction of structures and organisation charts. Despite their appearance of solidity, no doubt relating to the fact that they are relatively easy to understand, to put into writing, and therefore to develop with a mere stroke of the pen – at least in theory, since we then arrive at the problem of implementation – they are still a long way away from the reality of those involved. The fact that such theories are preferred can have dramatic consequences to the extent that managers feel that by working in this way they are doing something useful, while those directly concerned are convinced that nobody is interested in what has meaning for them, that nobody is really listening to them.

In fact, action which focuses *in priority* on structures relates to intellectual routine, and does not therefore in itself produce change. On the one hand, we know perfectly well that we can give an organisation 20 different structures and finally have a high continuity in the methods of functioning; on the other hand, as we will see further on in this book, modifying the structures is not in any way a preliminary to true change: usually, it makes do with being the statement *ex post* rather than *ex ante*. It relates far more to 'active inertia', than to a true action of change.[10] Such inertia means that one is only interested in what one is used to seeing, hearing or talking about. A memo, a follow-up letter, the publication of a new charter are all part of the routines to which people no longer pay great attention but which fulfil the function of action, satisfying everybody until they are suddenly awoken by reality: for example, 'profit warning' in the United States plays the same role as sudden and uncontrolled strikes in France.

This is the way a major insurance company tried out when, at the time of a merger, it wanted to group together into a single entity banking activities which, until then, had been split between four different establishments, operating in several European countries. In one of these countries, already marked by language and cultural problems, this involved merging two banks, which were apparently totally opposed: bank A was perceived as being a 'bank for the wealthy', in which actors at all levels had wide margins for manoeuvre allowing free rein to their entrepreneurial leanings; bank B on the other hand, formerly a public savings bank, was looked on as a 'bank for the poor', displaying a management that was far more standardised, which its own members described as military.

In appearance, however, the *structures* of both banks were almost the same and resembled the picture that can be seen across Europe: division into regions, into areas, into districts and into branches. The objective drawn up by the person responsible for the merger and his team was, in a relatively short time, to arrive at an organisation that functioned in a uniform fashion, which was expected to legitimise the adoption of a new trading name, a new logo – in brief, a new image. These managers therefore threw themselves into drawing up a single structure, ironing out the few differences that existed between the two initial establishments and, above all, they started the development of a package of strict, complex and detailed procedures, intended to produce the uniformity of operation that they sought. The outcome was the development of a multitude of working groups, each created whenever a new problem arose. The energy involved was considerable and nobody had even thought about calculating the time spent on the process, so distant did this seem from everybody's preoccupations. Meanwhile, successful completion of the merger – that is, harmonisation, bringing everything into conformity with the general model – appeared to be the guarantee for the success of the operation.

After a few months, the first anxieties came to light: first of all, nobody seemed able to ensure overall coherence across all the projects and sites. These had been started up without anybody knowing either the exact number or topics; also, on-the-spot observations that were carried out from time to time demonstrated that everybody had their own individual way of doing things, so that what should have been a procedure of integration actually turned out to be a disintegration of the new entity. The more rules were made specific and restrictive, the less the local actors appeared to care about them, except to highlight their abstract and inappropriate nature to their managers.

What had happened? Once again, *real organisation* had raised its head. A survey carried out as requested by the managers rapidly brought to light the fact that, in the traditional system, particularly in bank A, the key duo, which in fact shaped the bank's reality, was that formed by the district manager and the branch manager. The first, responsible for the application by the second of directives and policies drawn up by the bank, in the conventional system had a few margins for manoeuvre which were quite useful in negotiations with the operational manager. Not only was he involved in appraising the branch manager, but he also had a function of supporting him with regard to commercial policy and, even more important, a possibility of adjusting the objectives fixed for the branch in line with his appraisal of specific situations. The relationship between these two partners was therefore deep, but at the same time varied and thus in contradiction with the path to uniformity followed by the new team.

When the new organisation was put in place, with its package of structures, rules and injunctions intended to produce the *non-differentiation* that was so sought after, the stakeholders had not accepted without grumbling the move over from the situation of *actors*, which was theirs in the previous system, to that of *factors* to which they now found themselves reduced. Everybody took hold of the new standards and used them, not in the way intended by those who had issued them, but in line with their own situation in the local game. Identical rules only ended up creating different systems and, as the bank's general manager remarked philosophically after the presentation on the results of this work: 'for the mechanics, we were good; but perhaps we neglected the human aspect'. The problem is that one does not exist without the other, and that an action for change focused on the first does not make it possible to anticipate or control what the second proceeds to do with it. Never has the expression 'putting the cart before the horse' had so much meaning, never has the reversal of priorities been so blatantly obvious with all its related consequences in terms of wasting human and financial resources.

CHANGE THROUGH PLAY ON ATTITUDES

So, does this mean changing *attitudes*,[11] in the most usual sense of the term – the way in which people express themselves and behave *individually* in organisations? For example, when it is a question of adapting the

organisation to the new demands of customers who are increasingly in
a position to impose their wishes, is it simply, or even principally, necessary
for those who are in contact with these customers, and who rarely even
represent a majority of the organisation's members, to change their way
of being? This vision of things, described in this way, reminds us of
Courteline.[12] One would switch from agents, from uncommunicative and
disagreeable employees, to actors who were smiling, quick, devoted, above
all wanting to render service. Such an approach, which could easily be
described as naïve, is nonetheless omnipresent in modern organisations. Of
course, for certain of these, it represents a necessity, a first essential step
towards a different conception of the relationship with one's surroundings.[13] It sometimes interprets the transition from apprehension of such
surroundings in terms of threats from which one must protect oneself, to
acceptance of a more open, more trusting relationship with one's contacts.
To be brief, it may express the organisation's 'sense of service', where we
will also observe that it is very different from country to country.

But, at the same time, such a vision of change does not lead very far, and
it aims above all at laying the responsibility for adapting to new constraints
on the only members of the organisation in contact with its surroundings.
In the same movement we see the appearance inside organisations of
familiarity, use of the first name instead of the surname, doors left open
and relaxed dress, as if the *container* of inter-individual relationships
could determine their *content*.

There is nothing like that, of course. The effects can even be reversed, so
much does this confusion place responsibility for the necessary changes on
the only personnel in contact with the public, thus further increasing the pressure on them, but without the organisational mechanisms that would help
them in this. Staying with this case of relationships with one's surroundings,
there is little chance of the smile becoming a competitive advantage, so
much has courtesy become the universal norm and aggressiveness the
exception. However, there is nothing in this way of changing attitudes to
indicate that the organisation has changed *in its reality*, in its methods of
functioning. A quick example, bringing us back to the tax administration
mentioned above, allows us to check this: during the period of tax declarations, the offices of this organisation are crowded with taxpayers seeking help
in writing their declarations. But they only open at 9 o'clock in the morning
and, as we have been able to observe, even when it is raining, people queue in
front of the offices. When the door is opened at the proper time and some taxpayer or other shows his irritation, he is told – politely – that the office was
not able to welcome them in! The individual attitude is faultless, the result
in terms of quality perceived by the 'customer' is catastrophic.

THE NEGATIVE ATTITUDE OF INSPECTORS

But we need to go further than this simple anecdote, and show in what way the reduction of an organisation to the sum of the individual attitudes of its members, or of some of its members, can produce the paralysing and unexpected effects that we have just talked about. Let us return to the transport company that was mentioned in the introduction. It now finds itself faced with growing competition, mainly intermodal, especially in relation to its high contribution customers. In answer to their continual demands for more speed, more punctuality, more efficiency, the company has developed a technical tool that the whole world sees as providing remarkable performance. It has even 'adjusted' its office hours so as to offer its customers the regularity and reliability to which they attach a great deal of importance. And yet everybody seems united in acknowledging, both inside and outside the company, that the service that accompanies this technical excellence is poor and in any case nowhere near the expectations of passengers. In particular, the level of personnel accompanying customers on their journeys – the inspectors – who, as their name indicates, check that everybody is in order, show little enthusiasm for entering into contact with them and *a fortiori* for promoting the company through behaviour towards encouraging commercial openings. They even have a tendency to 'disappear' as soon as the situation becomes complicated, after an incident, a delay, a disturbance – leaving customers to look after themselves and thus provoking a climate of irritation which has often been highlighted by the press.

Of course, the company's management became worried, and arranged for these agents, as indeed for other categories of personnel, to take part in huge programmes for 'training on service attitudes' in which everybody is seen to explain and demonstrate the need to modify their way of managing relationships with customers in the direction of greater availability. However, these programmes were not a great success and did not have a huge impact on passenger satisfaction – they even added to the deterioration in the company's social climate, already marked by repeated social actions among the inspectors. Management interpreted this response as a very negative sign, showing, if proof were really needed, that these categories were closed to any change, and the agents themselves took refuge behind increasingly passive avoidance behaviours, only seeming to take an interest in an optimal management of their personal lives – in this case the possibility of going home in the evening as often as possible – and the continual rise in their financial gains, helped in all this by union organisations who were only too pleased to assist.

So what is the origin of the misunderstanding and failure in this attempt at change? Once again, a misapprehension of what an organisation really is, reducing it to a set of individual attitudes which have to rely on the goodwill – or in this case the ill will – of the actors involved. In doing this, we have not taken into consideration that this *reality*, which we see clearly, as we move forward, is a crucial issue of change and yet at the same time so very difficult to grasp and accept. Here, it is the complexity of the sur-roundings in which the inspector finds himself, his context, which has been neglected.

This complexity can be quick to assert itself in this way, immediately indicating that it corresponds to the *real organisation*, the one that needs to be taken into account in the process of change: the inspector is on his own in front of a customer whose needs can only be exacerbated when the situation becomes disturbed. Not only will he express a profound and sometimes aggressive discontent, but in addition he will be hungry for information allowing him to reorganise his time, let his friends know, and so on. However, it is the inspector who is accountable for everything that happens in the company without any possibility of passing on the responsibility for problems to other people, to whom the customer does not have access and about whom he knows nothing. As a humorous illustration here, when the company asks its inspectors to give information to customers, it might have just the same results by reversing the situation. One side has no more information than the other, especially when customers nowadays can use their mobile phones to obtain information that is fuller and more reliable than that available – with great difficulty and no particular guarantee of reliability – to the inspector.

In fact, the inspector, rather like his colleagues in reception, is living in a compartmentalised organisation, where each party takes decisions without worrying about their effects on other parties or even on the whole set-up.[14] Each of these decisions can be justified, legitimate, dictated by the desire to satisfy the customer, and yet its final result may be catastrophic. The same can be said of the choice between punctuality and connections that every transport company knows so well: when a train or aeroplane is late, must the others be made to wait so that those who are the victims of this lateness can catch their next means of transport? Or, on the contrary, is it important to privilege the network's overall punctuality, so as not to add lateness to lateness? Each of such choices can be justified. But however that may be, in the company that we are using as an example, not only is the inspector not informed, but he also does not know on what criteria the decision will be based. And when such criteria have been drawn up in common, which is sometimes the case, it is unusual for them to be applied, as those who are in charge prefer to keep their autonomy, their uncertainty, and therefore their power. An inspector who wants to keep travellers informed thus runs the risk of being overruled by a decision contradicting what he thought he could announce and justify.

The same can also be said for station masters who are assessed on the punctuality of departures from their station. So, when an incident occurs during a journey and the inspector asks the manager of the next station to call in the forces of order, there is little chance that his request will be heard and executed. Promises will be made to him but not kept, reinforcing his sentiment of isolation and abandonment. It is evident that the problems confronting these inspectors are a long way from those that a strategy for change, anchored on service attitudes, or even attitudes alone, would be likely to handle successfully.

What is revealed here, more fundamentally, is a non-listening mechanism, which results from the priority given to the rule on reality, or confusion between the two. Some think that by producing 'good' rules, they are doing their work and they devote all their energy and intelligence to this; others feel confusedly that something is wrong, but find it difficult to assess the situation: first they do not have enough distance for that and second, if they had this distance, it could sometimes be dangerous to make reference to it. For in all bureaucratic environments, the universalist and egalitarian rhetoric condemns all sense of identity, and therefore adaptation of the rule, even if this is, on a daily business, the condition for the organisation's survival. Doing something is good. Saying something is to expose oneself to reproach in the case of a problem. One cannot expect actors placed in this situation to always live it positively. This explains a few explosions – less easy for unions to control when they themselves are far from the reality.

In the case under discussion, an incorrect interpretation of what an organisation really is, the hasty and protective simplification, the more general refusal of complexity, are going to produce unexpected effects: results which not only do not correspond to officially designated objectives, but which also aggravate the wrongs that they are supposed to remedy. In the situation we are looking at, one could call this the 'vicious circle of discontentment'. The less the inspectors are taken into account in certain decisions, for the reason that they do not directly concern them – confusion between appearance and reality, ignorance of the systemic aspect – the more they are persuaded that their company is rejecting them, which is no doubt false in human terms, and yet true in organisational terms. However, it is that and only that which counts for actors who always have more of a feeling for what is real than those who manage them. This results for them in behaviours of withdrawal, of non-investment in work – for which in addition they are severely criticised, with the backing of surveys on real time of work. In such a context, when their 'attitudes' are called on to palliate the organisation's inadequacies, they come to the conclusion that they are being made fools of, and use their situation of strength to always ask for more, particularly in terms of organising their personal lives, their working hours and time off. In brief, they play on protest as compensation for organisational ignorance, supported vigorously by union organisations who are only too ready to capitalise on such conditions.

ACTORS WHO ARE NARROW-MINDED? OR INTELLIGENT?

This is how conservatism and immobilism flourish and prosper in these organisations, where everybody complains that it is impossible to get them to move forward, but where everybody passes the buck. On one side, management departments attribute the failure of attempts at change to agents who are themselves particularly attached to their privileges and to their union organisations, which feed on this in the proper sense of the term;[15] on the other side, the personnel concerned are made extremely suspicious by the fundamental lack of knowledge of organisational reality shown by those who are inviting them to change. There is often only one way out of this sort of situation – a crisis with all that that entails in the way of dramas, financial and above all human costs.

We will have the opportunity to return to this case in more detail, in particular when evoking the possibilities of changing the way the cards are dealt. But for the moment, it offers us a different vision of what an organisation is, of what must be the focus of all attention when things are to be changed. And you will probably have understood from the above, we are going to reflect that an organisation is first and foremost *what the actors do*, in other words, their *strategies*. We are not going to look at the whole demonstration, in theoretical[16] as well as practical terms, we will simply, by means of a few simple 'flash-backs', try to see the consequences from the point of view of controlling change.

The first is blatantly obvious: it is, by definition one might say, far more difficult to change the strategy of actors than to resort to redefining the structures, definitions of functions, processes, or to call on their good sense and goodwill. Applied to the case shown above, this implies that changing the transport company – which we are using as our guiding thread – means first of all ensuring that the inspectors stay with the customers or be in a position to stay – when needed. Consequently, if the organisation is seen as a set of rational actor strategies, it is these actor strategies, and not attitudes or structures, that it will be necessary to change. The challenge is considerable.

It makes us look at the human being, not from a 'humanist' view of things or out of a form of generosity, but because this factor is at the heart of the problematic. It represents the substance of what we seek to transform. It does not make things easy for anybody.

But the word 'rational', as used above, will make the company extremely complex. In fact, it does not mean that actors make the right choice – the only one possible – that they don't make mistakes, or even that their actions are approved. It implies the *intelligence* of such actors; that is, *their ability to find a solution acceptable to all in their existing context*. We have all, at some point in our lives, experienced situations where we have tried to convince somebody else to act differently, generally without success. The resulting annoyance has led us to interpret this person as being blinkered, narrow-minded or even not concerned with the general interest of those around him, with that of the company or any other form of community. We were simply in the process of discovering that the intelligence of actors means that, in organisations as in everyday life, we never convince anybody. Of what use is it to explain to intelligent actors, who have found an answer that is more or less suited to the situation in which they find themselves, that they must act differently than they are acting now? You might as well explain to a child who is punished each time he brings poor marks back to the house that he must *nevertheless* continue to do so. It would be if he obeyed such instructions that one should be worried about him. The word 'nevertheless' is used here in desperation, in order to lead the child to accept the dissociation between his context and what one wants him to do, make him admit in some way that he must relinquish his intelligence. This just shows to what extent such human intelligence is a problem in our organisations. We are faced with it each time we send a message – a vision – that is contradictory to the context in which the actors have been placed, usually by these same managers who are expressing the vision. Intelligence is what causes the actors to adapt themselves to the context rather than to the message. It is, at the same time, very demanding because one cannot 'say just anything to just anybody', and also very rewarding because each of us, in our place, always has the possibility, however modest, to modify the context of others, therefore to act on their behaviour. Such identification of 'margins to manoeuvre', always wider than expected, comes from investment in knowledge.[17]

This observation of the intelligence of actors not only goes against conventional elitist perceptions, but will also partly change the vision that one can have of management in general: if one defined it in simple terms as the ability to get people to do what one wanted them to do, then it is neither by conviction, nor by pressure, nor by appealing to common sense, to reason or to sentiment, that one will obtain it. To formulate this more harshly, it is not by intentional or unintentional manipulation, which from the point of view of action changes nothing, that one can influence what the actors are doing, and hence change the organisation. Or at least not in the long term, since although, at the time, everybody can succumb to surprise, give way to threat or panic, adjustments inexorably will be made as soon as the context allows. The only result from this type of action will have been to augment the distrust of actors, their protective behaviours, their life-saving routines. As soon as we distance ourselves from the reality, human systems have all they need to make us pay dearly.

As a result, changing organisations, especially in an environment that is always more demanding, requires qualities that are different from those that we are used to utilising. Conviction is certainly needed, not just to 'win the day' but to show that one has really listened; that is, understood the reality of the actors to whom one is talking. It is necessary to appeal to their goodwill, but only on condition that the words are in agreement with the acts or, in other words, not contradictory with the context in which the actors happen to be placed. It is striking to observe, for example, that an ever-growing number of managers are convinced of the need for cooperation in order to improve the efficiency of their organisation, at the same time as they continue to appraise their staff on a strictly individual basis. Here again, the order fizzles out, at the same time that it damages the credibility of the person issuing it.

In a word, the primary quality, apart from the necessary modesty in understanding the rationality of others when this does not correspond with our intellectual models, is the ability to accept what is concrete, to see things as they really are and not as one would like them to be. This ability can be acquired, it can be worked on, it requires an intellectual investment in acquiring new modes of reasoning – and not continually referring to prescriptive models – which will make it possible to look on reality with a fresh eye, which will ensure that one does not rush towards quick solutions as demanded by managerial rhetoric, but instead looks carefully at the problems. This word is not used here with its usual meaning of the trouble or difficulty which confronts an actor, but in order to designate the profound organisational mechanisms which make it possible to understand and explain the real content of situations that we have to face and that require change. It is the opposite of 'symptom' and not peace.

2 The Process: From Symptoms to Problems

The following scene takes place during a factory visit to an automobile equipment manufacturer in the American Middle West. This unit is mainly involved in the manufacture of various models of radiators on two production lines, one of which, the factory's pride and joy, has just been completely restructured. Our guide is a young engineer, brilliant, enthusiastic, volubly and accurately explaining the whole production system, the reasons for the almost clinical cleanliness of the workshops, the way in which staff meetings are held at the end of each shift to report progress, the absence of intermediate stock – which he considers to be his best success, even earning him a mention in the company's newsletter. In brief, an idyllic picture, which confirms the first overall view glimpsed by visitors.

INTERMEDIATE STOCK AS SYMPTOM

The production process itself appears simple, which again the young engineer reckons to be a success. Huge metal rollers at the head of the line unwind at a regular pace. The sheets are pulled along by the belt, passing under successive chambers where processing is carried out. The finished product is immediately removed at the end of the line, as the factory follows a pull production system. A relatively low number of operatives watch over operations in an atmosphere redolent of calm, conscientiousness and concentration. One might just happen to notice that the line has an 'elbow' bend – a 90° angle three-quarters of the way along its length – because of the size of the workshop, according to our guide, who does not seem to attach much importance to it.

And yet, if one stays to watch alongside this 'elbow', one of the operatives can be seen, standing inside the right angle, his back turned to the incoming flow ... and nonchalantly leaning on a pile of 20 or so half-finished radiators. This is pointed out to the young engineer, asking if this is not one of those famous build-ups of intermediate stocks which, as industrial history has shown, have the extraordinary ability to reappear just where they are least expected, and no matter how sophisticated the control equipment is that is used.

21

Beyond the first moment of surprise and, one has to say, embarrassment faced with this visual observation in contradiction of the theoretical plan, the unit foreman's reaction is to rush over towards the operative, and hurriedly ask him to account for what has just been discovered, thanks to our presence. The operative does not seem unduly bothered by what is said (he must be about 20 years older than his manager), and calmly explains that this is in fact a buffer stock, but this really doesn't matter because, officially, in the data which are carefully collected at the end of the line, these radiators do not actually exist. He has, he says, taken them over time, without the operation being accounted for. Honour is therefore saved, appearances respected and there is no need to make a fuss about something of so little importance.

HUMAN INTELLIGENCE AS PROBLEM

This response produces a completely different effect on the young engineer from the one expected by the operative – he once again starts to re-explain the whole theory of pull production, the justification for zero stocks, and so on, to the workman who listens with half an ear. While watching the scene, we observe that the operative's position, worked out down to the last detail and from which he cannot in any circumstances deviate, does not allow him to see what is going on behind him. Some questions directed at the engineer enable us to understand that each person working on the line has the possibility and even the duty to stop it if there is a problem, generally a defect on a part going by on the belt, or an interruption in the supply of parts. But interrupting a line, especially in pull production, is a serious action, which will subsequently require explanation. Before making such a decision, the operative will want to be certain that the incident really exists, will talk to the workman before him on the line, actions requiring a minimum of time, and which are therefore only possible with the existence of a buffer stock.

Certainly, this workman is intelligent, and there is no way of convincing him to act otherwise for as long as his surroundings are arranged as they are. But our young engineer has leapt onto the solution – explaining to the operative why he is wrong and what he must do. In his haste, he has confused the *symptom* – there is an intermediate stock – with the *problem* – how to protect oneself in a context which sees the conjunction of pull production, of drastic quality management on the chain and the physical positioning of the operative isolated in his 'elbow' corner. It is in fact a rational strategy for the operative to protect himself in such a context. But the confusion between the two dimensions (symptoms and problems) paralyses any action, renders dialogue impossible and, without our involvement, would no doubt have rapidly led to a conflict situation.

In wanting quick action, in hoping to find immediate solutions that will avoid us seeming to be 'slow', 'intellectual', not very dynamic, in being too quick to jump to conclusions or, in other words, to believe anecdotes rather than facts, we are making a mistake. And, especially in terms of change, the mistake is costly. It generates a whole series of unexpected effects that are often difficult to control, which are the price that organisations make us pay for *ignorance*. And, in parallel, it paralyses in advance the action of those in charge, who intuitively hesitate to take risks when faced with a situation that they feel that they do not control. It is therefore never the right moment for change, and one then finds oneself confronted with the syndrome of crisis.

WHAT IS A STEP IN THE PROCESS OF CHANGE?

One must therefore accept the need to lead change in steps, the first of these being, as we have seen, to dissociate symptoms from problems. And yet this idea of steps is itself open to debate, especially as, to start with, it reminds one of the conventional action plans, in which the phases succeed each other in accordance with a carefully pre-established order and tempo. This type of action adheres to ritualism, and it is always the most conservative organisations which are most likely to use and abuse it.

Placing himself at another level, Edgard Schein, a great specialist in organisational therapy writes as follows: 'this notion that I must first collect data in order to plan a subsequent intervention is, I now understand, one of the most senseless ideas in the field of consultancy'.[1] While the idea that diagnosis and intervention must be conducted simultaneously and not sequentially is certainly attractive and relevant when this is a therapeutic approach, it does however need to be adjusted once this involves managing a process of change, which one does not necessarily wish to result in a destruction phase prior to reconstruction.

And even if one must avoid falling into the *process* of change, the best way of producing immobility, there are *moments* that stand out more or less distinctly from each other and which avoid the 'precipitation' which has become such a sign of our times, as noted by James March. 'Unfortunately,' he writes, 'we are engulfed by the contemporary enthusiasm for an immediate solution ... our enthusiasm has become excessive'.[2] It is therefore important to keep a place for what he calls 'research knowledge', as already demonstrated by Chris Argyris to be the very condition for action, provided such knowledge is not just useful, but also usable.[3] This general acceptance of knowledge being a prerequisite for any action, at least in the worlds of universities and consultancies – since it is still under debate by current managerial rhetoric, as well as by companies that make it a point of honour to ask their managers not to think – is what we call here the transition from symptoms to problems.

WHY THIS TALK OF 'SYMPTOMS'?

This medical metaphor is not used by chance, since we only take an interest in change when something comes to our attention. In the same article, Schein writes:

> we need to start with symptoms, with irritating data, with programmes gone up in smoke. There can be a variety of metaphors, but it is self-evident that true change only occurs once the organisation experiences a true threat or real pain. Such pain can be felt in the form of culpability, when one recognises that certain values or ideals have not been achieved. The goal can then be a real improvement, even though it is still based on a tension between what is desired, and what is perceived as being the present reality.[4]

Even so, the pain must fairly severe and, as highlighted by this same author, 'the anxiety to survive' must be greater than 'the anxiety to learn' for, as we have continually repeated since the start of this book, reality is frightening and knowledge is disturbing. And no doubt the solution is not found in a dramatisation of the symptoms, in an attempt to cause alarm faced with the seriousness of the problem, but rather in a reduction of anxiety faced with learning. This is far more widespread among management than among their subordinates, as the acceptance of learning is primarily a 'posture' signifying the acknowledgement that one does not know everything, or that one did not know. But is one a true manager when one doesn't know? This brings to mind a senior manager saying to his Executive Board in introduction to the restitution of the results of a diagnosis that we were going to present: 'if one of you says "*I already knew*", I shall consider that as serious professional misconduct'. There is, therefore, a need to demonstrate that the knowledge of problems is not atagonising but in fact quite the opposite, since it allows one first to talk to others and second to control the results of what one is undertaking to do. Again according to Schein, this is one of the conditions for 'intellectual security'.

In order really to understand the distinction that is proposed between symptoms and problems, one can reassert this in all the debates around 'knowledge management', in other words, the capacity that organisations have to build themselves up from knowledge and to pass it on. Knowledge that is unrefined, spontaneous, intuitive, however important it may be, does not form a corpus that can be transmitted as is. There is a need for work to be done on processing it, analysing it and interpreting it, to ensure that what is communicated has added value in terms of the initial sentiment of actors. This also makes it possible to capitalise on practices, systems in operation, and not just on anecdotes. These must be separated from the facts which lead to an in-depth understanding. To summarise, the symptom can be considered as an item of *information* and the problem as an item of *knowledge* bringing one to the conclusion that the problem is an item of *information understood*.[5]

THE UNDERSTANDING OF PROBLEMS AS A LISTENING MECHANISM

This has major consequences in terms of change, and in the first place on what listening really means. Taken in its first meaning, listening simply means asking actors their opinion on such and such a question, or their hopes and expectations. This can be applied to a company's employees as well as its customers, and the methods used will then be those of a survey, attitude studies or 'corporate barometers'. The implicit postulate is that what actors have to say on reality, including their own reality, is a true reflection of this reality in all its complexity. Replies which are then made will be 'linear'; that is, they will correspond point by point with remarks made by actors, customers or employees.

Experience shows that such an approach can lead to catastrophic results, completely the opposite of those looked for. What actors expect, when they talk to those who are there to listen to them, is that they will help them to understand what is going on, why they do not feel at ease or why things are not as they would like them to be. Of course, everybody has explanations that are more or less well founded, supportive and compartmentalised and seeks to promote them. But if one comes back towards the actors, merely returning to them what they have said in a more or less ordered fashion, they will have the feeling that they have not been listened to, even that one is trying to use their words as a pretext. To summarise this into a formula, *listening is not asking people what they want, it's telling them.*

There is, of course, nothing manipulative in this way of saying things. It simply takes account of the fact that actors have an initial perception of reality, which is not enough to take into account the complexity of the situation, which is not an item of information that is understood. In the transport company mentioned earlier, we caused a surprise reaction from one of the managers in the following circumstances: when questioning him at length on the inspectors, he used an insulting term to speak of them, emphasising just how much he considered this category of staff to be unreliable, even dishonest in their behaviour towards the company. We queried the harsh severity of his judgement and he then explained how unfair it seemed to him for these people to use any pretext whatsoever in order to always ask for more, and always to be prepared to go back on strike once these additional advantages had been granted to them. We pointed out that such behaviour was, to the contrary, a very clear sign and, when he showed his extreme surprise, we suggested that obtaining additional material advantages was no doubt not the problem, but much more a symptom. In a way, these officers had done their work by going on strike, and it was now up to him to do his work in understanding why. The true need is there and this is why knowledge is frightening to start with.

Symptoms, these *misunderstood pieces of information*, show themselves in various ways. They are the organisation's *events*. Sometimes they are technical and involve breakdowns, delays or a sudden increase in the costs of non-quality; at other times they may be financial and show themselves in a drop in profits, a fall in turnover or a loss of market share; in human terms, they may take the form of high absenteeism, repeated strikes, or employee claims that are never satisfied. And the one-off or sequential response has little chance of sorting things out – in fact, quite the opposite.

For actors have a partisan interpretation, in the strategic rather than polemic sense of the term, of the symptoms which show themselves. It is for this reason too that the absence of in-depth work, in transforming information into knowledge, brings pointless conflict into the search for solutions.

An interesting example serves as illustration: during a survey carried out a few years ago on establishments taking in mentally or physically handicapped children, researchers were moved and impressed by the devotion of all the people working in such establishments, in emotionally difficult conditions, bearing in mind the serious handicaps that were being dealt with. At the same time, a persistent problem marked the life of such institutions, generated by the virtual impossibility of personnel to develop a collective 'establishment project'. And yet they were all in agreement: the interests of the children, especially those who were handicapped, must not be affected by political in-fighting and should be the subject of an easily obtainable consensus. When looking closely, however, it seemed that each person realised all at once that the children's needs were not always sufficiently taken into account (the symptom), and gave, to the defence of the interests of these young inmates, a definition which, if it had been applied, would have ensured the pre-eminence of their profession over the others within the establishment. The doctors gave priority to treatment, the educators to teaching, the psychologists to individual monitoring, and so on. Their good intentions were never at doubt, it was simply that they only had access to partial and biased information, which did not help them to reach agreement on the true nature of the problem to be dealt with – the extreme complexity of the situation of these children, which would have required from them a very constrictive cooperation compared with the segmentation and specialisation of their jobs, to which they had become accustomed and for which they had been trained.

THE TOOLS FOR LISTENING

There is therefore a need for investigation and, without entering into too much detail on tools which have been presented elsewhere, we are now going to discuss and illustrate some practical applications, with a view to highlighting some of the problems.

The first point looks into the transition from the *occasional* to the *complex*. Generally, indeed, a symptom is one-dimensional. It highlights one part of the organisation, the behaviour of one category of actors, it points the finger and the projector on what is seen. In fact, it allows appearance to be apparent. But a simple re-formulation, in the following terms: 'When such and such an event takes place, which actors must be taken into account in order to try and grasp the true nature?', makes it possible to go beyond the initial simplicity. Here, this involves tracing the *sociogram*; that is, *the representation of the relationships between actors, as experienced by the actors themselves*. This makes it possible both to effect a first illustration of the *system* which forms itself around the identified symptom, and to look at the positive, negative or neutral aspects played by the actors in this system. We will then move on from these relationships to the issues and strategies that underlie them. By remaining at the level of the symptom, we were focusing on the *apparent* actors; with the sociogram, we will be focusing on the *relevant* actors. Here is a practical application, which brings our guiding thread back on track – the transport company.

You will remember that the main symptom attracting the company's attention is the generalised behaviour of avoidance practised by the categories of personnel who are in contact with customers, mainly the inspectors, when in a difficult situation. It is to face up to this commercially punitive situation that the company has launched its training programmes on 'service attitudes', aiming to change the attitudes of employees toward customers.

The implicit assumption is that, in this case, only two actors are involved in the relationship, those who are visible – the inspector and the passenger. These are what we call the *apparent actors*. When these same actors are asked to describe their working universe and to evaluate the relationships that they have with the '*rest of the world*', they give a view which is far more complex and which would become even more complex if all parties concerned were asked to express themselves. Schematically, this universe can be represented as in Figure 2.1.

A few explanations are necessary in order to understand Figure 2.1 from which we will see that this alone provides a comprehensive interpretation of the reality.

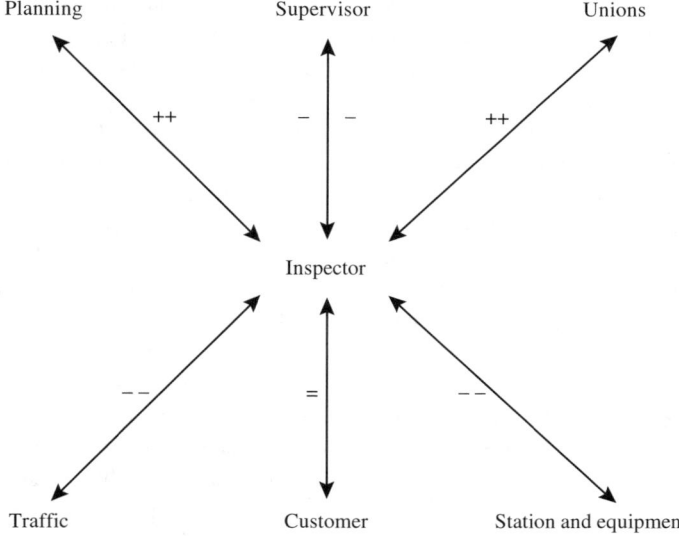

Figure 2.1   The world of the inspector

UNDERSTANDING AND CONTROLLING COMPLEXITY

The inspector lives in a universe the complexity of which goes well beyond the simple face-to-face with the customer, with whom he has, in effect, a relatively neutral relationship – particularly in a normal situation when such a relationship boils down to checking travel documents, carried out as quickly as possible. With his boss, the supervisor, relations are stretched: the inspector considers that his line management is of no help to him in his daily life and even less so in awkward situations. He is alone to face his surroundings with a distant boss who cannot give him the necessary information, nor help him to resolve his immediate problems, which above all have a bearing on his relationships with other actors. In addition, he bitterly reproaches his bosses, themselves former inspectors, for having 'forgotten everything', and for having taken refuge in a passive application of the rules, a long way away from the reality of work, and which means for example that he will be appraised on his appearance, general presentation, and so on.

'Traffic' is a key actor, which will help us to understand the systemic complexity. In appearance, its relationship with the inspectors should be distant, even nonexistent: they belong to two quite distinct company departments. Traffic deals with regulating traffic flow, ensuring safety and continuity and above all, as needed, it makes crucial arbitrations between punctuality and connections, based on criteria which, as we have already noted, are vague, if not nonexistent. Inspectors blame them for this lack of transparency and, when they occasionally need to contact them in dealing with an urgent situation, they emphasise the very dubious reliability of the information obtained. When questioned in depth, traffic officers, for their part, seem to be unaware of the very existence of inspectors, who are not part of their working environment. They have a technical perception of their work, marked by an obsession with security, which means that the customer, in the materiality of his daily problems of punctuality, is not a concrete preoccupation for them.

Under the general designation of 'station and equipment', we find, on the one hand, all the actors contributing to preparing the means of transport (cleanness, lighting, heating, arrival at the station on time) and, on the other, all those involved in receiving, directing, informing customers in the station, including the sale of tickets. Here again, the inspectors emphasise just how little care such actors show in their work through a multitude of anecdotes, certain of them being well known to the company which carefully files them under the heading 'return of experience', which seems to signify that there has been a problem and that, for once, it was known. This concerns technical infractions, involving the way in which things were done but not taking into account the reports, apparently many and varied, sent in by the inspectors. The officers in charge of equipment, if one only listens to them, defend themselves by saying they do not read the reports, of which they even deny the existence. As for those allocated to selling tickets, they carry out their work under pressure from customers who are always in a hurry and consequently not concerned with asking too many complicated questions. As a result of this, there are discrepancies between the tickets sold and the journeys made, which might lead to a conflict situation in the relationship between customers and inspectors, if the latter did not prefer to refrain from checking tickets in such circumstances, even if this means that the company loses money.

As its name indicates, the planning department is in charge of fixing how inspectors are allocated, in accordance with extremely complicated rules which have given rise to the development of an impressive set of regulations, intended to ensure everybody's equality in terms of workload and working constraints. One can fully understand the importance of this function for an itinerant population, often concerned with carrying out the shortest possible shifts – those making it possible to go home in the evening. Here, it is not the rule which makes this possible, but the *accommodation with the rule*, which is negotiated directly with planning officers without the need to go through any sort of official procedure. One can understand why inspectors find their colleagues in the planning department to be friendly and obliging. One will see, in passing, that this *power* which conditions the life of such staff is not held by line management, and this gives us an idea of the extent of the confusion, within the company, between organisation and structure. On one side we have rules which are supposed to plan for and organise every situation but which are endlessly broken in order to allow life to follow its course, and on the other we have bosses who have no real hold over this life and who therefore hide behind formality and ritualism.

There are many union organisations and they are even more active when in competition for this population which is a key actor across the whole company, since legally transport cannot take place without the presence of inspectors on board. The result of this is continual bargaining, continually renewed negotiations, which sometimes lead to a surprising feeling of absurdity: in this way, it has been necessary to reach agreement on the average number of steps that an officer takes per minute, in order to determine whether the fact of going into a hostel at the end of a journey was part of the working day or not! When questioned on the subject, the inspectors express doubts on the real knowledge that unions have of their daily lives although, with nothing better available, they nonetheless appreciate obtaining additional advantages through their intervention. As for the unionists, truly a state within the State, they have the monopoly on access to top managers, who only communicate through the unions in accordance with mechanisms and rites that no one ever questions. In addition, the human resources department has a good number of former militants among its ranks.

If one now wanted to get this sociogram to 'speak', although one should bear in mind that it is only a tool, one would note first of all the extreme complexity and diversity of the *relevant* universe in which the inspector exists, and which has little to do with the official structure to which the organisation chart links him. Even better – for him, his boss is not a important part of this structure.

One can then see that the actors with whom he has the most strained relationship are those who affect his professional life, whether upstream or downstream of his work – those who plan the journeys, sell the tickets, make important choices. However, these actors themselves act outside any anticipation of the consequences of their acts and their decisions on the face-to-face contact between the customer and the inspector. At best, they are not bothered, at worst, they think of him as a nuisance, and are not far from sharing their doubts with management on his true involvement in work. Even if they wanted to take things differently, the company's official organisation would make this difficult. The absolute and sought after segmentation does not push towards this, and does not make it possible finally to leave the narrow confines of one's own action, which leads all those involved towards a sort of resigned fatalism faced with the observation that what is happening is neither wanted nor decided by anybody whatsoever, it is simply *there*.

On the other hand, the inspector lives a very positive relationship with the actors who participate in the organisation of his private life, who allow him to choose his way of life, like those who negotiate his benefits for him. It would not even be necessary to push the analysis any further in order to understand, at least in general terms that do not enter into the detail of the mechanisms, that the less interest the company, *in its real method of functioning* and not in its statements or its intentions, is able to take in the professional life of its officers, the more they take refuge in their private life, to which they pay an almost exclusive attention. Starting from a symptom, that inspectors do not stay with customers in a difficult situation and reduce such relations to a minimum in a normal situation, we are not far from having understood the problem, simply by looking at the *relevant universe in which they evolve* and which is a long way from their theoretical and hierarchical context of action.

FROM ORGANISATIONAL COMPLEXITY TO
SYSTEMIC COMPLEXITY

Even in such a case, the complexity is reduced by the fact that all the actors are evolving in the same structure, which makes their identification easier. But sometimes it is necessary to face systems that are more complex, that are not bordered by any visible frontier. Michel Crozier and Jean-Claude Thoenig gave a brilliant illustration of this by analysing the French political and administrative system in its local operation.[6] With a lesser degree of complexity, it is the same reasoning that can be used in the following case of a company producing non-durable consumer goods. It calls in an outside consultant to help it remedy what is not right in its purchasing department. When the consultant asks to be able to carry out the interviews which are the stock in trade of his work, the company replies by telling him to feel free to question anybody and, for this purpose, they provide him with an organisation chart of the purchasing department, which includes a department head, product managers, to the extent that this company makes very varied purchases, and finally buyers. One can already see that the answer, which seems simple and logical, nevertheless contains a postulate with heavy consequences – that understanding what is happening within a *structure* can be reached *from simply taking into consideration the actors in this structure, which of course is not the case.*

Once again, passing via the symptom is going to prove fruitful. Questioned on what was causing it to cast doubt on the effectiveness of this department in this way, the company emphasises that the buyers are always buying more packaging items, the basic product which it uses. Despite repeated training courses on 'pull production', on 'just in time', on 'lean production', their behaviour is recurrent, stocks are inflating, which represents a not insignificant cost for the company. The managers have even started to wonder about the ability of the buyers, incapable of assimilating mechanisms which are nonetheless simple. But for the consultant, this indication is going to make it possible to ask the question in other words – which are the actors who enter into a relationship at the time of buying items of packaging, and what is the relationship of these actors?

More simply, a first look around makes it possible to identify three particularly *relevant* – the buyers themselves, of course, but also the production manager who is in charge of stock management, and finally the suppliers, who are obviously important. It is evident that these three actors come from different environments – different structures. The buyers and the production manager belong to the company but not the same

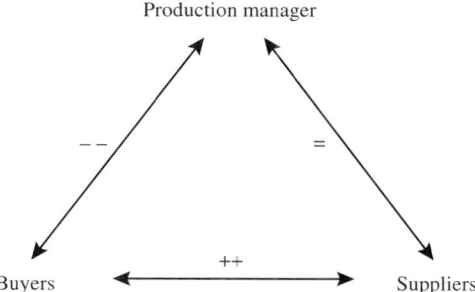

Figure 2.2   The relationship between the production manager, the buyers and suppliers

department; as for the suppliers, they are totally external. The picture of their relationship gives the result shown in Figure 2.2.

Buyers and suppliers get along without difficulty, appreciate each other and sometimes even admit to friendships outside work. The production manager is very critical of the buyers who return the coin with interest: the former reproaches the latter for their irresponsibility which leads to a costly inflation of stocks, while the latter cannot forgive the former for his eternal dissatisfaction even with really low unit purchase prices. Finally, the suppliers and the production manager do not know one another and even ignore each other.

WHAT IS 'METHODOLOGICAL REALISM'?

Figure 2.2 helps us to see that there is a strong alliance between suppliers and buyers and a no less consequential opposition between buyers and the production manager. These are splits which do not match at all with official designations. The very idea of the system is in contradiction with notions like that of an organisation and its environment, because this starts from the actors, it *listens to them*, it rebuilds their reality and not the theoretical universe into which the organisation chart places them. And it is this *methodological realism* that will make it possible to draw up the analysis which must follow, which will lead to the disclosure of the *problems*. In the present case, the questions that appear focus on the nature of the alliance between suppliers and buyers and on the motive for the opposition between these buyers and the production manager. These are alliances and oppositions that analysis will show to be of a strategic nature,

Actors	Problems to be solved	Resources	Constraints	Strategies

Figure 2.3   Analysis grid

that is, linked to the interests of actors and their intelligence, while the first interpretations by managers presume the reverse, even casting aspersions on the morality and honesty of their troops.[7]

Once the complexity in which the actors are evolving has been taken into account and their relationships defined, we need to analyse the system that has been revealed. It is this process which allows us to move on from *information* to *knowledge* – to understand the information that has been collected. The conceptual context will be strategic reasoning, and our tool the analysis grid, shown in Figure 2.3.[8]

In practice, when its use is intended to reveal problems, some points merit more particular attention. By actors, one should understand relevant actors, individually or collectively, as previously defined. Their conceptualisation is not always immediate. Some of them are discovered during analysis, either because other actors mention them repeatedly, or because the systemic reasoning leads up to them. We must again remember that there is no formal 'frontier' holding them together, and that their relevance is defined from the symptom or symptoms that provided the starting point for analysis. From this point of view, such a concept invalidates even further, if possible, the idea of structure, which is only rarely relevant in terms of change and which even obscures the view, especially when it is this that is looked at first in any inquiry into change.[9]

THE KEY POINTS OF STRATEGIC REASONING: SOME REMINDERS

These actors have problems to resolve, not in the usual sense of the term of a sudden difficulty which occurs (missing one's train, for example), but in the sociological sense of what they seek to obtain when they do what they do. In addition, they are *intelligent*, which has the result that *they decide to resolve the problems in the realm of the possible*. This observation is both one of the most difficult to grasp, and one of the most useful in terms of change. Indeed, in our first perceptions, when we are reflecting on the actors' problems that need to be resolved, we tend to do this in the abstract by projecting onto the situation under consideration what we think the actors *should* be seeking to obtain, or what we would be seeking to obtain if we were in their place. But we are not in their place, and however hard we try, we never will be. An actor's intelligence leads him to reason on the means before establishing the ends. He perceives his context, what we later call resources and constraints, and, based on this appraisal, he seeks to achieve something that is within his reach. This, in fact, is why lessons or morality or appeals to good sense have little effect on him and are therefore not vectors of change. This observation is a long way away from the usual rhetoric of management wanting to convince somebody tackling, with his bare hands, an adversary armed with two revolvers, that courage – or motivation in managerial language – consists of trying to get hold of the weapons! In such circumstances, the actor will establish the problem as saving his life and will adapt his strategy to this by running away.

On the other hand, however demanding this may be, this perception of action, which relates to what we have called *methodological realism* opens up enormous possibilities in terms of action. For, once one is in a position to modify the actor's context – what we will be calling *leverage effects* – this actor will adapt the problems that he is trying to solve to the new situation created in this way and will modify his strategy as a result.

From an analytical point of view, this means that it is more advantageous to look at the resources and constraints of the actors, than to rush into an abstract and disconnected definition of the reality of the problems to be resolved. By resources, we mean what the actor consciously or unconsciously assesses as being usable; the constraint or constraints designate what the actor anticipates he will have to face in his action. Both of these which can be material items (rules and procedures, for example) as well as other actors, form the context in which he finds himself and to which his intelligence will help him to adapt. But still from the practical viewpoint of moving over from symptoms to problems, if the little grid suggested here is used properly – it is of course only a means, a tool, and not an end in itself – *then these symptoms must appear in the matrix*, as either resources or constraints for the party involved, or as their strategy, a concept defined in the previous chapter.

This is what makes it possible to *build knowledge*, moving from the statement, 'in this organisation we observe that this happens', to 'this is happening because this element is an essential resource for this actor, and his strategy consists of acting on it in the following way'. Starting from a technical apprehension of the symptom – a late delivery, for example, or a regular loss of customers – one could go as far as its interpretation in terms of methods of functioning, which is a prerequisite for any reasoned action.

THE PRINCIPAL RESOURCE OF THE MOST POWERFUL ACTOR

The following example gives concrete form to the reasoning developed above.[10] A company producing a mass-consumption product is on the point of being privatised, having been a public enterprise since its inception, benefiting on its national territory from a monopoly in manufacturing and distribution. Even though the number of factories has been reduced over the years, the general organisation has remained the same: a head office, which everybody considers hypertrophied, located in the capital, and factories all operating in accordance with the same model, applying to the letter an impressive package of standards, rules and procedures drawn up scrupulously by the industrial division with regard to production methods, and the human resources division for everything to do with the management of individuals. In each of the factories, production is carried out in workshops comprising three categories of personnel – on which we are going to focus our attention, leaving to one side the management team. The shop foremen, with little in the way of qualifications, arriving there on criteria which have nothing much to do with their technical competences, but much more to do with the tradition of providing them with a second job after they have taken retirement, simply watch over the application of rules upon which they are very dependant. They are in fact production accountants who do not invest themselves very much in work. They are paid a fixed salary with little likelihood of progress, which they seem to adapt to without any great difficulty; the production workers either drive the machines, or handle the raw materials and finished goods, switching between these two functions every fortnight. Their wages vary and depend, to a significant degree, on the level of production that they achieve. In the event of an incident on their machine, they lose a proportion of their 'bonus', even if they are in no way responsible for the breakdown. Finally the maintenance workers, highly or even over qualified in relation to the requirements of their task, carry out the calibration and maintenance of machines, especially when there are minor breakdowns. If these become too serious, the repair work is entrusted to an outside company. In addition, they control the union organisations, in which they find themselves alongside their production colleagues.

The thing that worries senior managers on the point of facing up to competition, is that they are seeing a breakdown rate that is substantially higher than that seen at competitors, as well as average call out times on machines for small incidents that are again higher than the business average. Training programmes have been set up with the intention of making all categories of personnel aware of the problem and strengthening the already impressive competences of maintenance staff. The results have been very disappointing, with no significant improvement seen. The company, therefore, decided to have a diagnostic review carried out by a specialised outside consultancy.

The presentation which has just been made makes it possible to anticipate the principal results: the maintenance staff are the dominant actors of the 'workshop systems', since they control what is a decisive factor in the reality of power – they control a relevant uncertainty as orthodox sociology might say – that is, machine breakdowns, on which the production workers depend for their wages. This observation is not banal, as it allows one to understand the *organisational aspect of a symptom which appears as a technical aspect*. One might say that, in such a case, the breakdown is not simply a machine that stops – a very impoverished vision of reality – *it is the principal resource of the most powerful actor*.

The difference is not slight in terms of action. In the first case – the technical vision – the solution consists of repairing the machines and giving even more training to those whose task it is. In the second case – the organisational vision – wanting to reduce the rate of breakdowns in order to adapt to competition, this means reducing the power of the dominant actor, which is quite another matter and far more difficult to manage.

This is the reason for which, even when remaining very cautious faced with any overhasty generalisation, we will see that, as soon as one has identified the principal resource of the most powerful actor, one has a good chance of putting one's finger on the key point of the system being studied. This is both an interesting open door for action (and it must be remembered when reasoning on priorities) as well as a datum to be handled with extreme caution, since one can be sure that an actor does not willingly give up something that allows him to dominate a system. Opportunity and difficulty offered by what others would call the *regulation of the system*: we have just glimpsed the heart of our subject.

THE SEARCH FOR AUTONOMY AS THE MOST UNIVERSALLY WIDESPREAD PROBLEM

Nonetheless, the thread must be pulled tight until we have a complete understanding of the symptoms. The shop foremen are not very 'motivated' and keep out of the day-to-day running, which management notes regretfully and impotently. But by reviewing the concepts that have been proposed, it can be seen that these actors who are supposed to be in a hierarchical situation, in fact have no resources but, to the contrary, a number of not insignificant constraints, in particular the abundance of procedures which deprive them of any possibility of decision and the fact that the maintenance staff do not report to them, but to an engineer outside the workshop.

Like all intelligent actors, they adapt their problem that needs solving to the context in which they find themselves – *in which they have been placed* – and simply try to live in peace. In doing this, they *transform one of their constraints into a resource* – which in the sometimes comical managerial language of business schools is known as 'managing an opportunity' – and hide behind regulations in order to avoid being forced to take action. One can understand that they have a strategy of withdrawal, in the same way that production workers seek to have the best possible relationship with *their* maintenance workers, at the same time as denouncing their arbitrariness in general. The latter, as is the case for all actors possessing a major resource, content themselves with using this with a view to preserving their *autonomy* which, as we will note in passing, in experience *is the most widespread problem that needs resolving in organisations*. They therefore play on the repair times of the machines – second symptom – in order to protect themselves against untimely requests for their intervention which might disturb their work, over the pace of which they intend to maintain control. As one of them says: 'no journey without destination'.

And so we learn that, in this small system, which was neither wanted nor created by anybody in particular, but has developed over time into its current existence, the breakdown is the major resource of the dominant actor who, because he is intelligent, uses it and thus inflates the length of time that he is involved on the machines. We have moved on from the symptoms to the problems, using a method of reasoning which, for reasons of practicality and transmissibility, we have formulated in the shape of tools that are easy to use. But, at the same time, the reasoning used, and the results obtained in this way, make it possible to revisit the problematic of change, by once again focusing on realism. For the technical perception, which legitimises the reduction in breakdowns, is finally that *aesthetically,* non-breakdown is better than breakdown. As a young MBA student said to us one day, particularly shocked after reading this case study, 'This organisation has got to be changed because it cannot please as it is.'

That may be true, but it goes without saying that, for as long as the company is in a monopoly situation, there is no real reason for touching anything at all, to the extent that the *extra cost* of *regulation* by breakdown is *externalised* onto a third party – the customer. On the other hand, adaptation to the new context, which forms the transition to a market economy, cannot take place through a simple change in structures or attitudes. It will presuppose – it has presupposed – a completely new deal of cards; that is, the fundamental transformation of the methods of functioning. And the analysis which was made helps to provide a better understanding of the issues. It is the *strategy* of the different actors that must be changed, putting them into another context, which they will probably not find it easy to accept, at least with regard to the maintenance staff.

This will presuppose that one does not try to plan everything or confront everything, all at the same time. It is going to be necessary to fix priorities. The preceding discussion makes it possible to glimpse how to conduct the reasoning that is going to fix them. At the same time, it is evident that changing strategies presupposes a different context – an emphasis on the resources and constraints of the different actors involved. These are the leverage effects. Here, we will see that the methodological framework, which we have just reviewed and summarised, is only very slightly contingent on the context that it allows us to study. It is a method of reasoning, which focuses on the why of action, which emphasises the importance of the context, no matter what the nature of this. The same can be said for the levers with one important shade of difference, that the *nature* of the levers used, their actual content, is, itself, contingent.

3 The Process: Looking for the Priorities

Knowing whether it is necessary to fix priorities or instead to decide on what is most appropriate to try in order to cover the overall problems identified, is currently being debated among the specialists on change. We have already noted that Schein considers that, from the moment of collecting information, one has already started on the process itself and that, therefore, there are no such things as *phases*, except at a very superficial level, where the action plan takes the place of real action. Similarly, there are many who criticise the idea of a succession of sites, in the name of the required simultaneity of action, which must help to prevent the creation, between different parts of the organisation, of variances which would later be relatively difficult bring back together.[1] No doubt they are right, if only because of the systemic dimension of organisations.

Intuitively, the majority of managers who have responsibility for major changes have adopted this viewpoint, and have always tried to have all events under control, by building programmes that are intended to forecast, right down to the smallest detail in terms of what might happen and what aspects must be dealt with in close-up or from a distance. This tendency makes itself particularly felt during merger processes which witness the creation of a multitude of 'steering committees', each in charge of a specific area concerned more or less directly with the merger. Such an approach is understandable in this case since there are very few of the different parts of an organisation that are not concerned, and above all because, in such circumstances, we see the appearance of legitimate anxieties concerning people's prospects and employment, which need to be dealt with without too much delay.

CAN ONE DEAL WITH EVERYTHING AT ONCE?

Everybody can see that the programme is quickly transforming itself into a number of sites where the natural tendency is to live more or less autonomously, without those who have been put in charge of their *coordination* – a term which clearly indicates that naturally the sites are separate from each other – being able to make the link between all the suggestions and initiatives, sometimes in contradiction with each other. Because of this, in the bank which was introduced in Chapter 1, it was necessary to call in an outside consultancy to compile an inventory of the different projects that had been initiated, assess their compatibility, and make proposals on withdrawing certain of them, modifying others, and so on. In brief, the management of sites opened for the merger became a more worrying problem than the merger itself, and progressively monopolised a high proportion of energy, until it was realised that the actors on the spot were forced to find practical solutions which were in fact far more interesting and useful than those from the *ad hoc* committees.

Similarly, in the transport company, even though it is not in the process of a merger, or visibly undergoing a major crisis, but in which the directors are supposed to carry out a true cultural revolution, the 'priority action programmes' have multiplied in trying to cover all aspects of the 'project', which gives the overall orientation and vision. The result is identical: the life and death of such programmes depends above all on those who are in charge and results in meetings, committees, memorandums – of which nobody tries to have a precise understanding. As far as their real impact is concerned, in real-life they produce the same effect as an over-abundance of procedures in any organisation: they make those in charge of applying them free to choose those that suit them best, which they use, producing the effect which has already been seen elsewhere: too much integration kills integration.

It is no doubt for this reason that, for years, the transport company has tried everything. No stone, in terms of management methods, has remained unturned. The culture of its managers and internal consultants is, in this respect, seamless. They have read everything there was to read, taken part in every colloquium, been part of every adventure. And yet, despairingly, nothing has changed, and the conclusion that the directors have drawn from this does not focus on the way in which change was managed, any more than on their real intention to make things evolve. It points a finger at who is to blame – the consultants who have made money out of the company. Yet managing these consultants was part of the management team's responsibility – in general and more particularly in the case of change.[2]

SYSTEMIC CHANGE DOES NOT IMPLY OVERALL ACTION

Such failures arise from the confusion between the systemic nature of organisations, leading one to consider that each part, even if identifiable, is linked to the whole, and the consequence which is hastily drawn from this that one cannot focus action on a single part without taking responsibility for the whole. In fact, *there is no contradiction between systemic reasoning and the idea of priority*. The first implies that the most effective means of action to change a part is not necessarily to carry out a linear-type action, while the second suggests that if one wants to *enter* into a process of change one needs to find the right door. The priority is to find the door, systemic reasoning is what helps you to open it.

And, in fact, if changing organisations means changing the strategy of actors, then one can understand that it is difficult, and no doubt unnecessary, to want to change all these strategies in one fell swoop. Such an attempt might bring Orwell to mind, and in point of fact the very idea of the intelligence of actors which is at the heart of our approach is in contradiction with Orwell's world, even if the end justifies the means. It is therefore necessary to find another logic, different from absolute planning, far from abstract and universal action plans, and accept a random element which at the end of the day is irreducible, since it concerns human freedom, which once more shows itself as a major difficulty in abstract and standardised approaches to management.

This random element which is so terrifying but inherent to every process of change, is impossible to predict and measure. Once the door has been opened, and even more important before it is opened, it is really difficult to know what we will find behind it, and to control those who will be rushing through it. This has a major consequence when one is seriously striving for a successful action – *the final result of the action must not be evaluated solely or principally with respect to the initial goals*. Proceeding in this way means 'cornering' those who are in charge of the process, it means artificially limiting their capacity to profit from new situations that arise, it means making the overall organisation blind, deaf, incapable of learning.

As in negotiation, the action of change structures new opportunities because, based on the priority which has been fixed and which it is believed will substantially modify the game, the actors have adapted themselves, have found new solutions, certain of which will need correction, but which to a great extent constitute the *spontaneous way in which change spreads*. We will therefore arrive at an extremely accurate steering path, which will be based on the actors themselves, rather than an attempt at the absolute control of the whole process which is in any case bound to fail. Here, what we call priority is not the most important, or even the most urgent problem. It is the part of the system on which one thinks one has the most possibility of acting (strategy of the possible) and where modification has the best chance of changing the functioning of this system, and therefore of launching and enabling the whole process. In most cases, this is what makes it possible to demonstrate to actors that nothing is permanently written and that it is possible to do things differently.

Nonetheless, the definition of one or more priorities comes up against a difficulty that, in the introduction, we called *the billiard ball effect*. One of the features of a system is the coherence of its component parts with each other, and researchers are well aware of this – sometimes falling back in admiration once they have understood the overall logic of their subject of study. They have the feeling that they have reconstituted a puzzle – and of course they don't want anybody to come along and move a single piece.

This is the 'fascination of the cobra' exercised on us by this systemic harmony, which means that its sometimes catastrophic final result runs the risk of being forgotten. In this case, as in front of the snake, one only seeks to remain motionless. The principle of reality however recalls us to action, but the difficulty remains in finding the angle for attack that will make it possible to lift the constituent contradiction of any action which takes place in this problematic: how to reconcile what is *desirable* (acting on what would be the identified priority), with what is *possible* (there is a reasonable chance that the phenomenon of resistance will not scupper the attempt).

Once again, this question is made even harder, in that what we are trying to change are neither structures or superficial attitudes, but the strategies of the actors. Of course, reflecting on *implementation* will also open up paths for us, but we will see that there is no ready-made answer to the question asked. Either, as has been suggested, the priority is found around the principal resource of the most powerful actor and one is going to come up against serious difficulties, or else the action is going to pinpoint on the edge of the system and its effects are not guaranteed. It is therefore each situation, in its specificity, which will make it possible to weigh the elements in play, for we have never been so far away from possible recipes, from 'devices', which would help us to avoid making mistakes. Nonetheless, through the two examples that follow, we are going to try to illustrate the two situations most frequently encountered: it is up to everybody to take them as examples and not as models.

THE CASE OF THE EUROPEAN DEVELOPMENT BANK

The first of these examples is in the context of a big financial institution in Southern Europe.[3] At the time of the survey – towards the end of the 1990s – this bank, in its 'retail banking' part, shows three *symptoms* that are worrying top management and that justify calling in an outside expert. The private and professional banking network is beginning *to lose money*, and even if low profitability is acceptable in this country bearing in mind the extremely sharp competition, the situation is showing signs of deteriorating beyond the business's limits. At the same time, one can see a *draining away of customers*, not in the form of a massive haemorrhage, but in a slow and regular movement mainly affecting the most profitable customers. This disaffection, which appears clearly in the statistics, is however minimised and even denied by those in charge of the network, especially the account executives, persuaded of the loyalty of 'their' customers, whom they manage exclusively, monopolistically, in a logic which, on observation, appears closer to that of independent workers than to that of account managers for a bank of this type; and yet, surprisingly, despite these first two negative indicators, everybody in the network *achieves their objectives without any great difficulty*, which shows that the anxiety manifested by general management is far from being universally shared by line personnel.

These three symptoms gave rise to much debate within the bank and interestingly one can see that it is not the figures that help the actors to come to agreement. Despite their apparent objectivity, they raise very divergent doubts, arguments and interpretations, thus reinforcing the bad atmosphere that reigns in the bank: everybody suspects everybody else of manipulating these figures and using them to their advantage. Above all, discussion rapidly becomes heated, so much are the actors concerned absolutely convinced that they are doing everything they can, without counting what they give in terms of their time and energy. There is nothing surprising in this: this is what actually happens in circumstances where the actors, focusing on the symptoms, cannot come to agreement on the problems.

What does analysis show, when one focuses on the four principal actors in this situation, the customers, the commercial advisor, the branch managers and the network management? In terms of the *relationships* between these actors, one is first of all surprised by the almost friendly closeness between the commercial advisors and *their* customers. With only rare exceptions – such as the few customers who indicate their doubts on the extent to which the products offered to them actually meet their real needs – everybody is happy with each other.

The account executives watch jealously over their portfolios which they share with nobody, not with the branch manager who in any case has no customers to manage, or even with their colleagues. When one of them is in need, which is a rare occurrence, the others help him – not by handing over customers but by transferring part of their results, even if this means manipulating the figures.[4]

As for the customers themselves, they are delighted if, by playing on the bank's poor image as echoed in the press, they manage to obtain, from their contacts, ever more discounts, rebates, and services not charged.

It is evident that account managers are assessed on turnover and not on profitability.

In contrast, one is struck by the absence of a relationship between customers and branch managers. When one interviews the former, they never mention the latter although, on the other hand, they express very negative opinions on how badly the bank is managed, for which they hold network management responsible. An account holder never misses an opportunity to emphasise how happy he is to have opposite him a contact who is capable of offsetting the deficiencies of an organisation that is heavy, bureaucratic and probably corrupt. But in so doing, they are referring to the account executives and not the branch managers.

Between the latter and those who are, in spite of everything, their subordinates, relations are ambiguous. Managers complain bitterly of the high level of autonomy enjoyed by commercial advisors, an autonomy which they feel little able to counterbalance, and emphasise to what extent they have no information on customers, the market and its potentialities and, more generally, on business within their branch.

The reporting system is sparse, quantitative and does not take real situations into account. It is not on such a system that the manager can rely in order to exercise any sort of control, nor indeed on his hierarchical authority to the extent that, since promotions within the bank have been blocked for an undetermined time, any judgements he may make on employees are without real effect. As for the account executives, they find managers to be relatively conciliatory and appreciate the fact that they do not hesitate to fight with financial management in order to obtain better physical conditions.

In its judgements, network management is strict with everybody. To the sales staff, it reproaches their practices aiming to favour the customers at no matter what price; it insists on their fanatical individualism which leads them to 'hide the copy' from the rest of the organisation, thus depriving it of the visibility needed for its own action. It has often organised meetings with the advisors, but these have proved to be unfruitful, strained, even aggressive. In addition, it deplores not being able to rely on its branch managers, that it perceives as over-scrupulous, always ready to say yes to everything, without anything ever happening. In particular, it does not succeed in obtaining from them any more information than it obtains from the sales staff. The assumption of complicity between these two actors is clearly evoked. To finish, management emphasises that this situation is all the more prejudicial in that it makes its own work, continually launching new products (some of which are the best on the market), defining new priorities every day, which are immediately transformed into new action plans. In brief, everybody bustles about busily for a disappointing result but with nobody perceiving the fundamental causes.

Such is the situation, described as seen by the actors. Analysing it allows one to brush out what is overall a conventional portrait of this organisation. It will have escaped nobody's attention that, in this bank, the person who has *the reality of power* in his hands is the commercial advisor. For this, he has a particularly important *resource* through his monopoly of access to the customer. With very little in the way of *constraints*, one can therefore understand the two *strategies* that he develops: first, the provision to his customers of ever more advantageous conditions in order to keep them captive; and second, the retention of information,[5] which, as we have seen, even extends to his own colleagues and which helps him to preserve his autonomy, which is no doubt *the problem he needs to solve*, in the sense that we have used it.

RESPONSIBLE BUT NOT GUILTY

Stopping a moment on this first observation, two points merit highlighting that are going to have all their impact on the form and content of a process of change. In terms of form, the method of analysis used avoids casting any direct or indirect blame on actors. Reasoning in terms of *rational strategies*, it is good to anticipate that it is these strategies that need changing, but it also means affirming that they constitute *an intelligent response from the actor to the context in which he has been placed*. Because of this, there is no apportionment of 'responsibility' in the sense of bad intention, and it therefore serves no purpose to argue at length on the crafty intentions of one person or another.

Better even, if one wanted to go into the details of this case, one would quickly see that, if customers have a relatively negative perception of the bank, it's not just because of the image given to it by the media, but also because the sales staff criticise their own organisation in front of the customers; they distance themselves from it, its heavy and bureaucratic 'back office', its incapable directors – and only think of their careers. In brief, in their commercial relationships, they sell themselves and not the bank, they manage the contact on an individual basis and not a collective one. In addition, this is not special to them as it is well known that the more one affirms living in a restricting and rigid universe, the more one seems flexible and adaptable in relation to one's contacts. Unforgivable, will say the moralist. Certainly, but here, what is at stake is the intelligent logic that the actor pushes through to its conclusion. And it is not contradictory with

the feeling that he has of doing everything he can and holding the bank's survival in his hands. At this stage, moralising criticism will only exacerbate the
conflict, just where the strategic approach makes it possible to insist on the
devotion of each person *even while* noting the final result which requires a
profound change.

Turning now to the content of the change process, we have just identified
the principal resource of the most powerful actor. There is again no doubt
that here we have the key point of our organisation, which will in principle
appear to us as the priority we are looking for, the one which, if we succeed
in dealing with it in a strategic manner as opposed to in a technical or authoritarian fashion, will enable us to unbalance this system which nonetheless
seems so very hermetic. However, even if this intuition has a good chance
of proving itself well-founded, it is not enough on its own to build the
strategy of change. The analysis must be pushed to its conclusion, partly in
order to find and identify other priorities that may exist, but also and above
all in order to draw up the reasoning on the levers to be used in order
to change the strategy of the actors, including that of the most powerful
of these.

This brings us to the branch managers, who appear to be singularly
destitute in this system. Not only do they have no control over the essential
source of power in this organisation – access to the customers – but also
they have no real means of action on the commercial advisors since they
do not influence either promotions, reduced to little if anything, or pay,
which follows rules which have nothing to do with them. In counterpoint to
this absence of resources, they suffer from the same lack of information as
the rest of the bank. In such a situation, wisdom – intelligence – consists of
protecting oneself, of not going out of one's way to seek conflict with the
sales staff who are more powerful than them, and even of participating in
the general opacity which characterises this organisation.

In fact, this is a situation of inverse dependency which is observed
frequently in bureaucracies of this type. The head depends more on the subordinates than the subordinates on the head, and this gap between formal power
and real power is far from being inconsequential. It leads the custodian of
officialdom to 'compensate' for his lack of organisational resources by
always asking for more financial resources. We had already observed the phenomenon, we now find it here. But it must be remembered that there are
something like 800 branch managers who, to a greater or lesser degree, adopt
the same strategy of 'always more', leading to the notorious vicious circle
of inflation and bureaucracy that these organisations know so well.

What can the network management do faced with these impenetrable
local units which maintain it in profound ignorance of the living reality of

the market, contenting themselves with ritualistically filling forms up with information without really knowing to what this corresponds. One can understand that protecting their careers becomes an essential preoccupation, which is not too obvious in this situation where ignorance of the real can always lead to taking the wrong decision or not seizing a good opportunity. This leads the team to a strategy than one can only qualify as extremist: in order to cover themselves, they need to start always more projects, more priorities, more action plans. It is movement which takes the place of action and, as always in such cases, the multiplication of activities is an exact translation of the obscurity in which each of the leaders finds himself. In this respect, one might speak of military or ballistic strategy. The less one knows where the target is, the greater the temptation to sprinkle widely in the hope that luck will help us to hit something. But in doing this, those who are in charge of implementation – the commercial advisors on this occasion – only have more freedom to choose what they want and decide what *their* priorities are within this heap of decisions that are not particularly integrated and are in fact often contradictory.

FROM THE SYMPTOM TO THE PROBLEM

There is no need to go any further in the analysis to return to the initial *symptoms*. It is indeed this that makes up the step that we have called the transition from information to knowledge, and which is made accessible by what has just been said. It is also important to avoid falling into the common trap, which consists, after an excellent analysis, of proposing an interpretation of the symptoms which has little to do with the analysis and which, most of the time, leads towards technical explanations.

Why is the bank losing money? Two reasons have appeared during the analytical process. First, we have observed that *in the context in which they find themselves*, it is a rational strategy for sales staff to offer always more advantageous conditions to their customers, so as to ensure their loyalty to them and not the bank and, second, we have understood that the less organisational resources branch managers have, the more financial resources they ask for – even to the extent of cheating on the truth of information used to obtain them.

But then why do customers, and particularly the more profitable among them, tend to leave a bank in which they have been able to obtain pretty much everything they wanted? We have noticed that, in order to preserve their autonomy, account executives do not share their information, nor therefore their customers, with anybody, not even with their colleagues. They prefer, rather like the brokers we sometimes find working in stock market trading offices, 'passing' the customer over to a competitor rather than allowing one of their own to benefit, at the risk of putting a spanner in the works for ending the monopolistic management of customers. As we have said, they manage the relationship on an individual basis and not on an organisational basis. However, this strategy does have a limit – it quite naturally leads to sales staff offering their customers *the products that they know and only those*. Contrary to appearances, this is not a lack of qualification – nobody can know all the bank's products – it is more an absence of strategic advantage in sharing one's customers. Of course, everything works for the best in an ideal world, provided the products that the salesperson knows are the products that the customer needs. As soon as a gap appears, then the good individual relationship is not enough to compensate for a weak offer, and the dissatisfied customer goes away, even if, in other areas, the personal relationship with their contact remains excellent. This situation tends to be more frequent where the customer is more sophisticated, with complex requirements, and where their profitability would have good chances of improving if the bank managed to satisfy their requirements, which the system, as it is now, does not allow.

Yet everybody achieves their objectives without difficulty? In fact, there is a double process of budgeting in this bank. The first is official. As soon as it is time to draw up the budget, the network's management decides on the main lines and then distributes them over the rest of the organisation. The reality is quite different. Placed in a situation of non-information, as described above, which we must remember is linked to the strategy of the sales staff, management seeks to obtain some reliable forecasts from the next level down – in this case, the area managers. Those who don't know better turn towards the branch managers who themselves turn to their own advisors. In brief, these are the ones who fix their own objectives, and one can see why they should have so little difficulty in achieving them, since it is easy, outside of any control, to underestimate them in the name of genuine caution.

THE CHOICE OF STRATEGIC PRIORITY

As can be seen, all the problems that have been identified behind the symptoms refer to a main cause which is certainly not unique – the account executives' strategy of retaining information. One can understand that, for them, communicating on the reality of what they do on a daily basis with their contact and which might, for the bank, be a crucial source of living knowledge, really means giving up their principal resource, and therefore their autonomy, which one knows to be priceless for the actors, especially in a context like this one where the possibilities of promotion are reduced to virtually nothing. By keeping the information they have for their own protection, they produce the 'chain reaction' which has been identified, and based on which it was possible to explain the initial symptoms. It is for this reason that *opening up the game of the sales staff can be defined as the priority*. It is not simply that this is the most important question – others, such as the information system, are just as important from a practical point of view – but it is from that point that the deal can be changed and that other actions will become possible. This is how a priority is defined as opposed to a comprehensive but 'flat' approach to all the problems that need to be handled.

At the same time, this *strategic* vision of priorities feels far less safe for managers than the one that consists of decreeing, from above and in a 'set way', all the actions to be conducted. The priority here is going to be the 'trigger factor', the one that will make it possible to pull the thread of change. For change, ultimately, is far more a thread that is pulled than a final plan that is put into operation. Action on a clearly identified priority after careful analysis leading to a secure understanding of the problems is going to open up the field of what is possible and reveal opportunities that the construction of an overly rigid plan will be forced to clear away. For we cannot repeat enough that, from the first step they take, *intelligent* actors are going to find new solutions, different and often unpredictable arrangements. They are going to negotiate their acceptance, structure a new game, all those things that even the best-informed planner has no chance at all of anticipating, since the scope of human freedom is wide and forces them to accept an ever-increasing proportion of random events.

At the same time, this is what makes it possible to go further. From this point of view, the action of change can be considered as the creation of *positive chaos*. The leader's role is not to reduce such chaos in the name of consistency of control or predictability. It is to render it acceptable to everybody, give it a meaning, reassure.

In addition, this approach through the strategic priority avoids focusing on the technical solutions which are so reassuring and controllable. In the bank's case, it is tempting immediately to reappraise the information system; that is, finally to favour the channels rather than what runs through them. The temptation towards technical solutions in organisations is as powerful as that which attracts towards the structures. But it comes up against a major obstacle which, as has already been said, lies at the heart of the problematic of change: despite all the attempts to finish with this obstacle, people are, and will always be, stronger than the technology that is put against them. More or less quickly, they have every opportunity to oppose a new system of measurement, or counting, of control. They know how to turn procedures, find solutions that are always renewed in order to conserve an autonomy that others are trying to take away from them without anything in exchange. In fact, changing the technology, like changing the rules and procedures in a linear and not systemic vision, does not generally produce durable change.[6] Both are costly (especially technical changes) at the same time as producing results that are cosmetic rather than concrete. However, by defining an organisation as a set of actor strategies, by insisting on the fact that changing means above all changing these strategies, we have largely oriented the search for priorities. These can *only be strategic*. The remainder fall within the definition of resources or, which is not negligible, of *levers*; that is, of what one will be using to change what the actors are doing.

THE SYSTEMIC ASPECT OF PRIORITIES

If we return for a moment to the bank case, this is even a twofold priority, *of a systemic nature*, which is proposed. Not only is it necessary to act on the commercial advisors, but also to modify the simultaneously withdrawn and inflationist behaviour of the branch managers. And if one wants to anticipate briefly what will be said of the levers, both can be conducted in the context of the same action, again based on a systemic reasoning which might be stated as follows: is it possible at the same time to make it more rational for the sales staff to share the information that they have on customers *and* for the branch managers to become for them a resource providing something other than always more financial resources? One can think of different solutions – here is the one that was adopted by the bank. It based itself on what conventional management terms 'the management of opportunities'; that is, the possibility of transforming resources into constraints. In this particular case, it was pointless to continue appraising sales staff on the turnover that they were earning, to the extent that they themselves fixed the amount that was achievable. It was therefore decided, taking inspiration from a current practice in American business banks, that over a period of three years considered as experimental, the advisors would be appraised on their 'capacity to cooperate', and their pay, with higher variability, would depend on this capacity. The problem of measuring this of course then arose, for which two criteria were chosen with all the safeguards thought necessary by those in charge: first, the amount of business that each advisor would pass on to his colleagues, compared with what he would deal with himself, and, second, the proportion of customers on which he would work jointly with other colleagues, with regard to those that he would manage on his own. Because of this, he would find himself saddled with new constraints and forced to arbitrate between his autonomy and his pay. As always in such cases, the actor tries to maximise both gains, but there is no doubt that his strategy shifts in the direction of greater transparency – a condition necessary for satisfying the new criteria of appraisal.

At the same time, however, while it was becoming more advantageous for account executives to share their customers and therefore their information, they still needed to be oriented towards the competences that they might need in order to satisfy the complex of customers. In addition, there was nothing to show that such competences were available within their branch. Everybody will have understood that it was to the branch managers that this responsibility for orientation was entrusted, thus transforming them into resources for the sales staff, to whom they now had something to contribute that was directly in relation with their concrete working problems. What was given to these branch managers was not *authority*, in the hierarchical and Taylorist sense of the term, it was something for them to control which was important for those whom they had to lead. It is called *power*.

In passing, this leads us to observe that one has, through this, brought the actors to play together, just where, in the previous situation, they were only interested in retaining information, or even direct opposition. It is this idea, that finally, in any social group, one does not win against the others but with them, that they tried to introduce into this company by creating solidarities between actors, where the earlier system was pushing towards withdrawal and isolation. The game has stopped being a no-score draw.

THE PARADOXICAL FORMULATION OF ACTION

A second example will allow us to show that priorities are sometimes more complex to highlight, first, because the action can take place in a less structured field than that of a well-identified organisation and, second, because systemic reasoning can sometimes lead to what might be called a *paradoxical formulation of action*. In more complex systems, composed of actors belonging to different units, the choices become less obvious, requiring more in-depth and more sophisticated reflection, more upsetting as well, which causes a good number of managers to take refuge in simple solutions based on coercive rules.[7] This is what we were able to observe in a case, already old, focusing on the public transport of goods by road in France.[8]

This expression, somewhat barbaric, describes the fact of someone with products to be transported (the consignor), going directly or indirectly to a road haulier rather than dealing with it themselves or using another type of transport. In such a case, we speak of transport for hire or reward – this is what is meant by the word 'public' – as opposed to transport on one's own account. This case takes place in France, a country in which this has always proved particularly risky for the public authorities to handle, bearing in mind the power to harm held by hauliers, regularly emphasised by strike actions that paralyse the country and even part of Europe.

Yet there is a need for change when one considers the number of people killed and injured on the country's roads, and the proportion of heavy trucks involved in such accidents. Those publicly in charge of the issue are in agreement in recognising that the high speeds of increasingly powerful engines is an undeniable and serious risk factor. Nonetheless, for the reasons evoked above, they can only tackle the problem with extreme caution, and when particularly serious events make it difficult to stand back and do nothing.

When action is unavoidable, its scope is formulated as simply as possible by the administrators in charge – this activity is subject to national and European regulations which cover all aspects, and in particular those concerning the loads carried and the work and rest periods of those driving. If an accident is due to excessive speed or driver tiredness, this means that there is fraud through non-compliance with the regulations, no matter what point of these has not been applied. The priority is then stated as follows: *since fraud produces accidents, if we reduce fraud then we reduce accidents*. Never has formal logic been imposed to such a degree as proof, even if, over the years, the inadequacy of the results obtained leads to its validity being questioned.

Systemic analysis makes it possible to formulate the problem very differently, in particular by resituating it in its real complexity. It is important to understand first and foremost *how fraud can be a rational strategy* for the actors involved, in the context in which they find themselves. For this, it is necessary to get away from the moral (fraud is not right), or legal (France is a State of law) aspects, and look at the strategic dimension of behaviours. If the consignor has chosen to ask a third party to deal with his shipments, this is because he believes that the advantages that he will gain from this will outweigh the disadvantages of sub-contracting. That is understandable: when questioned, he will reply that he already has enough constraints as a result of his own activity, without taking into account all those associated with a sector outside his own. In other words, the pressure which he experiences at the two extremities of his activity – his producers who are always on the limit of the lead-times allowed and his customers who are always seeking to reduce stocks – is in contradiction to strict observance of transport rules. However one wants to formulate this, what he is going to require from his service provider is flexibility or, in administrative language, bending the rules. This, in a world where competition is continually expanding, has become the one *competitive advantage* that a service provider, especially a small one, without commercial autonomy, can offer in order to differentiate themselves from competitors. But even one with higher margins of play, with a diversified business, will accept what is proposed so as not to lose the customer. Quite simply, if the risk is too high, he will always find somebody who is more dependant than himself to whom he can sub-contract the work, thus participating in the 'avalanche of fraud' which runs through this system. In this business, there are also true specialists, designated under the generic term of 'intermediaries'. Fine connoisseurs of regulations and good specialists who are very aware of the situation of those around them, they can 'turn' towards somebody who is in a position to accept, without too much discussion, something which, in the eyes of the law, is extremely questionable.

SYMPTOMS, PROBLEMS, REGULATION AND EXTERNALISATION

As we can see, this whole system, far more complex than it appears at first glance, *regulates itself* around fraud, accommodates itself to it, in fact a solution far more than a problem. But what makes this solution acceptable, by all the actors who are directly or indirectly involved, is that they bear only a minimal part of the cost. This is really the accident, with all that it involves in terms of misfortunes, and such things as the financial costs of claims, repairs, compensation. However, through the intermediary of the insurance companies, which do not really distinguish between the risks involved for heavy trucks and for automobiles in general, the extra cost of the arrangement around fraud externalises across all motorists, or the victims, as one might say. Such phenomena of externalisation are classic and well-known to economists.

Sociologically, the logic can be expressed as follows: the dominant actors in a system – here the diversified road hauliers and all the ancillary services – have a better chance of coming to an arrangement – fraud – if the cost can be borne by one or more actors outside of this system – in this case, all motorists through the intermediary of the insurance companies. The re-internalisation of such costs, when this is possible, is always an interesting trail to investigate.

Change, in such a case, means obtaining from those who drive the trucks that they do so less quickly. All things being equal, one has little chance of achieving this through repressive measures which will be diverted, one way or another, or challenged until they are dropped. It is better to try and change the context of all the actors which, in this case, means re-internalising the cost of their arrangements into the system that they form. One can measure the complete change of outlook. It is no longer a question of reducing fraud in order to reduce accidents, as logical reasoning led us to believe. Systemic reasoning has made it possible to *reverse the priority* and to understand that it is better to try to reduce accidents in order to have less fraud. This is what is meant by 'making the actors bear the cost of their choices', which has no other purpose than to put them in a situation where they will benefit from maintaining accidents at a level involving consequences that are supportable by them; that is, in any event lower than the previous situation. The mutualisation of risk, or the involvement of the whole chain of decision and passage of order in the case of an accident, as has been attempted, are all possibilities.

As we can see, the search for priorities is not an easy thing, even when guided by an apparently solid methodology. But above all, it requires a strong capacity never to accept what appears to be obvious, what results from logical intellectual construction – the notorious deductive 'since' – rather than from the sometimes extremely complex functioning of human systems.

4 The Process: From Priorities to Levers

As soon as the priorities have been identified, the question arises as to how to modify the strategy of intelligent actors, how to bring them to make other choices, to find solutions that are acceptable to them. This question is at the heart of the problematic of change, and all those who have had to manage the real and fundamental transformation of an organisation have had to confront it. Technical, administrative or even financial problems always find solutions. It is rare for them to represent major obstacles. But those that are commonly known as 'human problems' in everyday language, and which are in fact problems of organisation, are far more difficult to overcome.

THREE TRENDS FOR A MEDIOCRE RESULT

The expression itself is interesting. In organisations, the human is a problem, in the sense that he does not submit easily either to the overall rules, procedures and codes which are supposed to make him predictable,[1] or to the wishes of his bosses, however powerful they may be. Curiously enough, these bosses work hard at maintaining the illusion of their power, of their ability to steer the course of things, through their charisma or their leadership style. But it is not enough to explain to people what should be done for them to do it, nor to appeal to their reason for them to become reasonable. Unlike an accepted idea, the reasonable is eminently contextual; that is, subject to a partisan interpretation from the actor. In other words, what some people conceive as common sense, is not necessarily seen as common sense by those at the receiving end of it. This is probably what explains the three main trends that have been observable, especially since the end of the 1980s, in people's conceptions of action and change: these can be incantatory, coercive or linear, thereby interpreting the extreme difficulty in confronting such human intelligence, which we endlessly make into the core of the problem. These trends illustrate attempts to avoid taking it into account, to go round it, often in the name of general interest, of authority, of management, or of apparent common sense.

THE LIMITS OF BELIEF

Incantation is the most universally widespread practice in organisations. It is, even so, extensively acknowledged and accepted as a tool for guidance that companies do not hesitate to give a semi-religious tone to staff or management meetings when explaining their 'vision' and what needs to be done. More basically, the incantatory tendency now becoming rife in organisations is resulting in a subtle shift of semantics: when they talk of their 'strategy', by this they mean what they *hope to do* and not what they do. 'Our strategy is to be number one on our main markets' they say. In fact, this is an objective, a project, while strategy consists of the actions that one takes to achieve this.[2] This shift expresses the huge gulf which separates an intention from the concrete way of realising it. And so we have seen, still in the 1980s, a multiplication of 'company projects' or 'departmental projects' ... which, as their name indicates, were only projects and in fact, in many cases, never got beyond this stage. Ten years later, the tendency is the same – the promotion of 'fundamental values',[3] 'core values' which overall are praiseworthy and positive principles although for the most part somewhat remote from the effective practices of actors, including top management.

THE TORMENTS OF PROJECT MANAGEMENT

To illustrate this point, we can use a version of incantation that has caused, and that continues to cause, many problems to companies – project management. This consists, particularly in organisations structured by businesses, such as car manufacturers or their suppliers, of designing and producing products or parts of products cross-functionally, by temporarily associating with the project actors from the 'trades'; that is, the traditional vertical structures as inherited from the Taylorist system of thought. At the head of such cross-functional units, which are formed and unformed as dictated by circumstances, as is their vocation, we have the *project managers*, in charge of getting everybody to cooperate with a view to achieving the best possible result. Plenty of difficulties appeared, as soon as these project managers were asked to become 'leaders of men', capable 'of commanding their troops' – all formulas relating to incontaction far more than to action, which might produce the neologism of 'incantation', in which many people would be able to recognise themselves. And, in fact, as the obvious advantage for those who have been allocated to the project is to continue privileging the logic of their own trade – since this is where they are appraised and from where their budgetary resources come – they are going to stick closely to this and the project will continually see ever more delays, ever more defects, and everybody will be able to reproach everybody else for their incompetence, their unwillingness. Calling for cross-functionality as an absolute necessity in order to offer the customer quality at the lowest possible cost will never be enough to change the strategy of the actors. This is the harsh law of human intelligence.[4]

In this case, the question raised is not that of the project manager's 'charisma' or of his devotion until exhaustion in order to accomplish his task. It is a question of his power, of how he effectively controls those who have been allocated to his project and which will mean that they are going to have an interest in cooperating with him. It is not enough to know that he is the boss, but it is necessary to realise that this is a project. More generally, one issue, on which incantation has no bearing, is the observation that, in organisations, one has more to gain by cooperation than by opposition. So, for example, it would be naïve to think that racers in the Tour de France throw themselves into a fierce fight to carry off the top prize. If this were the case, only a ridiculously low number of them would finish the race. In fact, they share out the rewards, under the vigilant eye of the man they themselves call the 'squad leader' who makes sure that everybody wins something. For if the strongest won everything, without discernment, the whole system would put itself at risk. In order to survive, it needs the cooperation of all. But once the squad leader is no longer capable of imposing his law, is no longer in a position to 'control' the race, it becomes a free-for-all.

THE INEFFECTIVENESS OF COERCION

The temptation then becomes great to fall back on coercion and plenty of companies have not been able to resist this for long when the context has allowed it: because actors do not want to do what they are asked to do, let's try to use authority in order to make them – rather like the traffic policeman confronting an offending motorist. Of course, in such extreme cases, which are fortunately not part of everyday management, coercion can give results. And yet these will always be limited. It would not occur to anybody today to assert that prison eradicates or even reduces delinquency. Some even say that it increases it, through an effect of the system which might well be analysed with the tools suggested here. In the year 2000, one American out of 174 was 'living' in prison, and this proportion is continually increasing.

In organisations, coercion is expressed on a daily basis by threatening internal memos, increasingly strict and numerous rules and procedures, which all propose drastically to reduce the freedom of actors and to enclose their slightest deeds and acts in a clear, defined, non-amendable context. From this point of view, and despite the sometimes mollifying words that accompany them, the various and varied ISO standards provide an excellent example of this reasoning and these practices, as we have already pointed out.

In doing this, what one is seeking to curtail, to control, even to reduce in the military sense of the term, is the actor's freedom – their capacity to make choices that do not correspond to those stated by the organisation. This, in particular, is what happens when actors are asked to adopt a behaviour that is in contradiction with the context created for them. Instead of trying to adapt the second to the first, one steps up the pressure, the regulations, the repression, in the hope that these will steer those concerned to an unlikely acceptance. It is, for example, surprising to see the contemporary fad for 'cooperation' on the part of companies and managers who nonetheless continue to assess everybody on an individual basis. The result is simply catastrophic and some, in a reflection of the French tax authorities, even reach the point of drawing up 'cooperation protocols', as if this difficult behaviour, so constrictive and unnatural, could be regulated in a protocol!

Coercion is an impossible means of action, which only produces effects in the very short term, and generally when the work situation has deteriorated, thus depriving actors of alternatives. But their freedom and their intelligence (it can be seen that we do not have one without the other), are pretty well irreducible. Organisations are swarming with examples that show the extraordinary capacity of actors not to do what they have been ordered to do, if they do not perceive the interest of this. From this point of view, administrative environments are a gold-mine. On one hand, they reason only by coercion whether this is for their contacts or their members; on the other, tolerance for non-performance is extreme. On one hand, the arsenal of regulations and procedures is impressive – for its quantity – in its intention to leave nothing to chance and especially not to arbitrariness, on the other. the diversity of solutions and practices is remarkable. In parallel, it is almost impossible to change anything at all in these organisations – so inextricable does the tangle of issues created in this way appear at the end of the day.

LINEAR REASONING AND SYSTEMIC REASONING

The linear vision of change, while of a different nature, still follows the same logic. This consists, after having identified a problem, which is in fact confused with the symptom, and located the actor who is carrying it, and therefore the 'culprit', of focusing the action directly and exclusively on this actor. The key word for this type of action is *since*. Since A produces B and not C as he is asked, let us act on A to make him produce C. This is what we saw in the last example discussed in the previous chapter: *since* fraud produces accidents and *since* fraud is mainly perpetrated by small carriers who have no concern for the general good, let us focus on them an action which is both massive and coercive through the intermediary of new regulations defining how they must work *and not by creating a context in which they will benefit from working differently.*

This approach, that might be qualified as simplistic, refutes the systemic dimension of organisations. Not that it is not sometimes necessary to act directly on an actor in order to make him change – we will be looking at an example of this – but, in most cases, it is not by directly targeting the offending action, excessive speed for example, that the desired result will be achieved. Most frequently, in fact, it is in the environment around this 'problem', often among the other actors, that one will find the leverage for action. In other words, in the linear vision, one demands, by force if necessary, that an actor does something with the hope that this will resolve the whole of the problem or problems, while in the systemic vision *one puts him in the situation of benefiting from doing something*, at the same time as looking at the overall resulting effects which will not fail to show themselves.

ACTION BY LEVERAGE OR RECOGNITION OF THE ACTOR'S INTELLIGENCE

From this point, what will be suggested is, first of all, to play on the *levers*. By this, we mean *the component parts of the context of actors, which, correctly altered, are likely to bring progress to their problems that need solving and, thereby, to their strategies*. The physical metaphor of the lever is not without interest: it does indeed consist of applying weight somewhere in order to obtain a movement somewhere else, as opposed to what has just been said for the linear approach. Acting through the effect of leverage, this consists of changing the resources and the constraints, that both sides have in the system, so that they 'align' their behaviour accordingly, by wagering on their strategic intelligence and not by seeking to reduce it.

This does not in any way imply the idea that these same actors are going to accept the new rules of play easily and without discussion. Thinking that would mean having misunderstood the concept of intelligence. The levers used, as we will see, can be very restrictive and the term 'intelligence' does not refer to the fact of finally accepting a change because the necessity for it has been demonstrated to you. It is in fact the capacity to adapt to a new context. The question of resistance or acceptance must be dealt with at the time of drawing up the method of *implementation*; that is, the definition of conditions which make new solutions playable by those involved, often disturbing compared with previous situations.

This is particularly true when one is caused to give new constraints to actors, who will inevitably, at least to start with, reduce the margins of freedom and autonomy that they have formed for themselves, before finding new arrangements. If this line of reasoning is continued, we will understand the importance of this point: we have already pointed out that the identification of the most powerful actor's principal resource generally *but not universally* makes it possible to reach the core of the organisation and of the symptoms which set off the alarm. In such a case, the control of a powerful resource pushes the actor towards a radical strategy, without apportionment, turned towards the exclusive and non-negotiated defence of its own interests, to the detriment of the interests of others or of the organisation as a whole. In this situation, the lever will consist of creating constraints for him, in order to get him out of his one-dimensional logic and force him to negotiate, if only with himself, on contradictory imperatives, which will lead him towards finding new solutions – no doubt better balanced ones.

WHEN COOPERATING IS NOT RATIONAL

An example will help to illustrate this remark: a European airline has been undergoing a major crisis since the beginning of the 1990s. Not only is it facing very hard-line labour disputes, but also its results are deteriorating to the point that it is beginning to lose money on a scale rarely seen before in the business and which will lead it to immediate bankruptcy without vigorous financial intervention from the public authorities. Many studies were conducted in order to identify the causes of such losses (the problems), and among all those brought to light, there was one that particularly drew attention: to carry out the maintenance check, also known as 'interim maintenance', which consists of immobilising an aircraft for some ten days, twice a year, the company takes on average three days more than its main competitor. Calculations based on the number of aeroplanes in the company, the average number of passengers per flight and the average daily frequency of turnaround, show that these three days result in a loss equivalent to 540,000 passengers per year.

The question then arises as to where these three days come from, how 'performance is constructed' in a way. After investigation, one finds oneself faced with a classic problem of organisation: for understandable reasons of safety, the maintenance department is structured in divisions (we should remember that organisations often have the vocabulary of their practices), which divide up the different parts of the aeroplane that is undergoing maintenance. There is thus an engines division, an onboard computers division, a cabin division, and so on. When one observes how these units function, it is clearly apparent that time is lost due to very poor management of interfaces, a systematic lack of cooperation between the different divisions, which are more likely to oppose than to find mutual solutions. They are not even located in the same premises and none of them appears particularly bothered by this.

The first reaction from managers, shocked by this realisation, is to appeal to the good sense of all concerned, forcefully emphasising the collective interest of survival, and vigorously denouncing the fact that the company is being endangered by those of its members who refuse to cooperate. Numerous seminars and 'team building' exercises are organised so as to bring people closer together, teach them to know each other better, all of which seems an elementary condition for working better together. This is the incantatory phase which does not give outstanding results. Questioned individually, most of the actors declare themselves ready to cooperate with their peers, but remark that these do not seem to be similarly inclined. In a word, everybody would like but nobody does.

It is therefore necessary to get away from this psychological and guilt-inducing approach and reformulate the question in strategic terms, following the framework that has been suggested. The symptom is clear, it is the three days 'on top' needed to carry out the interim maintenance. But the query on the problem is as follows: why, in the system as it is, do actors not see the interest of cooperating? And, on what levers could one act in order to bring them to work together, without having to give them a moralising talk on the superiority of cooperation in relation to distance and non-cooperation? Analysis provides a simple answer and without any great originality. For reasons of safety as mentioned above, each division is appraised on the number of incidents affecting the part of the plane for which they are responsible (rate of computer breakdowns for the computer division, for example). Each division therefore finds itself focused on its own work, which it devises independently of the others, to which it pays little heed. As a result, the total maintenance time for the aeroplane is not the problem that anybody is expected to solve, it is seen as remote and theoretical and, in any case, not as a concrete constraint that is really felt by the individuals.

Once again, they adapt themselves to the context, not the words. The one-dimensional and vertical nature of the criterion for appraisal leads to the one-dimensional and vertical nature of the action by actors.

BRINGING ACTORS TO ACKNOWLEDGE THE COMPLEXITY OF REALITY

It appears necessary to give them one or more constraints, which bring them to acknowledge other elements of reality. The problem is not so much to get them to move from one vision to another as to get them to assimilate several and bring them to arbitrate by finding new solutions. Of course, the result for them will be a less comfortable universe, precisely because this involves arbitrations, choices and, more concretely, new ways of working with others. It would be up to the actors themselves to discover these new cooperations, thanks to the 'constraint of constraints'. In the precise case that we are looking at, two criteria for assessment have been crossed: the one in force previously, still for the reasons of safety already mentioned, to which has been added, for all divisions, *the total maintenance time for the aircraft*, whatever the incidents that may arise during the check.

If we now take a step backwards, we see that the usage of levers has changed over time, no doubt under the impact of the growing complexity of situations that managers are asked to manage. To start with, it was simply a question of getting an actor to move from strategy A to strategy B. Playing on a simple element of the context – pay, for example – can successfully produce this effect.

But today, what is increasingly expected of those who are in a position of responsibility, is that they acknowledge the plural, contradictory and conflictual nature of action by integrating, not one, but several logics. This puts them in an uncomfortable situation, with which it is difficult to live, and which is part of the development of working conditions already mentioned. To obtain this result, we therefore use several levers – combinations of quantitative and qualitative criteria for appraisal – which will bring the actor towards finding an optimum between two or more logics and not the exclusive triumph of one over the others.

In a football team, when forwards are only assessed on the number of goals they score and are put in competition on this criterion, their advantage is certainly to score, but also not to favour the effectiveness of their partners. If one takes the 'assist pass' into account, it then becomes advantageous to be not just the scorer but also the one who makes it possible to score. And what can we say about the American basketball teams and their 'triple double' which leads to recognising, for each player, the number of points scored, the rebounds captured and the assists made. In this case, the levers bring the actors to the maximum degree of collective action.

These more restrictive conditions under which they are placed raise protests from the actors concerned. In the case of the airline, they emphasised the injustice which consisted of making the fate of one side dependant upon the goodwill of the other side and of appraising, and therefore remunerating or promoting, people on something which, at least in appearance, did not depend on them. But management held firm, basing its decision on a campaign of in-depth information which showed actors the harmful effects of the previous situation, without however putting them at fault individually. Little by little, the maintenance staffs adapted themselves and eventually presented their supervisors with proposals for organisation making compatible the criteria for appraisal which had been imposed on them and which they had until then seen as incompatible. Not only did they suggest that a certain number of operations on the different parts of the airplane could be carried out in the same place, but they also showed that they could take place at the same time.

To summarise, the lever used allowed them to move *under their own volition* from the sequential compartmentalisation characterising the traditional technical bureaucracies, to the simultaneous cooperation which, in all areas of production, is the principal factor for reducing costs and improving quality. This, in fact, is what happened in this case and one might note, in passing, that this fundamental transformation of the organisation, resulting in substantially improved results and having encouraged the actors to make considerable changes to their working methods, was carried out *without touching the structures*, and without requiring changes in attitudes. Structural adaptations were carried out *at a later point* when they were simply a confirmation of a state of being. They did not therefore represent an additional anxiety for actors, having been, in a way, made part of their daily life. With regard to attitudes, without entering once again into complex sociological debates on attitudes and behaviours, the example shows that these are a consequence and not a cause and that attacking them in priority is of little benefit, or even the major disadvantage of 'theorising' and pointlessly introducing conflict in the debate on change.

TWO LESSONS TO BE LEARNED FROM THIS EXAMPLE

This example of levers that have been used advisedly shows two important lessons to be learned.[5]

- It emphasises the huge importance of human resource management systems when conducting change. By human resource management systems, we mean all modalities of appraisal, of promotion, of pay, of career management, in other words everything that affects the well-being and future of individuals at work. It is these systems that conceal the highest number of opportunities with regard to the levers that can be used, simply because the intelligence of actors leads them to adapt themselves to the criteria on which they are assessed, appraised, promoted, remunerated. However, these criteria still need to have *concrete effects*, meaning that their satisfaction, like their non-satisfaction, must involve positive or negative sanctions. If this is not the case, as in the administrative sector, they remain theoretical and have only a slight effect on real behaviours.[6] This poses a question of *coherence* as already mentioned above, which clashes with the traditional segmentation of organisations. Human resource management departments draw up systems without an exact understanding of the reality – problems – or even independently of the results that they are trying to achieve. However, on one side, having a 'demand' in relation to the actors and, on the other, creating for them, via the criteria, a context that is not coherent with this demand, does not so much cause problems to the actor who will be able to accommodate himself and play around with them, as to the organisation which will never be able to control – in the sense of master – the effects of systems that it has put in place.

- It reminds us that one of the main changes affecting organisations today is the transition from one-dimensional universes to multi-dimensional universes. Such a development can realign the distinction made by Peter Drucker between manual workers and 'knowledge workers'.[7] This transition is seen in the fact that there are few actors who remain in contexts of 'mono constraints', who can continue to have a narrow and segmented vision of action, excluding both cooperation with others and acknowledgement of the final result achieved. In the same way that the structures of organisations become increasingly fuzzy and complex, despite repeated calls for simplicity, so do the environments in which the actors evolve become ever more diversified and contradictory. Calling for more simplicity, more clarity, is appealing and reassuring although, finally, rhetorical, unrealistic, once again incantatory, to the extent that the complexity is simply consubstantial with the need for multiple collaborations in modern businesses. But, from the point of view under consideration, this complexity must be translated into the levers that are used to modify actors' strategies, without being afraid to put on to their shoulders the constraints that will persuade them to integrate contradictory elements

into their action. Experience shows that they do this very well. In other
words, existing complexity rehabilitates conflict.

DIFFICULTY IN IDENTIFYING THE RELEVANT LEVERS

Nevertheless, the above case only gives a partial idea of the difficulties
there are, in most situations, in finding and using the right levers. And in
fact, the intention was merely, by taking into account only the actors concerned, to create a new context for them, without also having to look at
their environment. This situation is not the most frequent, even if it is the
most tempting, and the levers to be manipulated are mostly situated outside the precise field of the actors themselves. We will therefore be talking
of *banding effects*, by reference to the successive shocks of billiard balls
which finally cause the last ball to go where the player wants it to go.

The transport case discussed in the previous chapter introduced an idea
that can now be explored more fully. We showed that, in order to reduce
the speed at which drivers were driving, it is relatively ineffective to push
an extremely repressive action directly on to them, to the extent that they
are dependant and lacking in viable alternatives. In so doing, one only
adds new constraints to those that are already leading them to the strategies that one wants to amend. One thus increases their situation of dependency, and therefore their vulnerability with regard to other operators in
the system, who thus find it all the more easy to manipulate them. Using
this lever even produces exactly the opposite effect to that wanted: the
more that drivers, whether independent or on the payroll, are deprived and
restricted, the more likely they are to accept any sort of transport job, and
therefore sidestep the rules, which will lead the public authorities to regulate this activity even more severely, and all the conditions will come
together for an endless vicious circle. In fact, this is more or less what
experience has shown over time.

On the other hand, the systemic analysis that has been carried out,
because it has made it possible to understand the problem, and because it
has highlighted the 'inverted priority', has suggested that it was by acting on
other actors that one could modify the strategy of the road hauliers. This
banding effect leads one first of all to focus the action on the order givers,
the consignors or their agents, the ancillary services, even if their main characteristic is not to carry out the transport themselves and, *a fortiori*, never
even to drive a truck! And in fact this is why the competent authorities do
not know them – administrative segmentation is a virtually insurmountable
handicap for the systemic apprehension of reality and therefore for the

apprehension of reality alone. And yet, by involving these actors, who find themselves upstream of the transport, in the downstream consequences of decisions that they take officially or unofficially, one can hope to bring them to change the pressures that they apply to the drivers, even if, as should be remembered, their capacity to adapt to the new context created in this way will be high.

LEVERS, BANDING EFFECTS AND RE-INTERNALISATION OF COSTS

In addition, the concept of *externalising costs*, as already discussed, has allowed us to glimpse a more complex phenomenon: reintroducing the cost of the accident within the 'transport system', making the reduction of this cost the collective 'problem to be solved', particularly for protagonists who until now had not suffered any consequence. This leads to action by the intermediary of an actor whose importance has only appeared at the end of the reasoning process – the insurance company. It is this that, through its methods of functioning and of calculating premiums, allows the whole system to regulate itself around fraud. One can see that by acting on this actor, based on the mutualisation of road transport risk or any other form of calculating premiums, the lever will finally put pressure on all those who decide things for which they are not prepared to assume the consequences. And this new and *indirect* constraint will come and relieve their natural propensity to make use of the situation of dependency in which the lowest members of the chain find themselves, in order to preserve their most profitable markets.

We can discuss the feasibility of this solution. In particular, one cannot help but see that reducing fraud to a level that will generate fewer accidents runs the risk of resulting in an increased mortality rate among businesses operating nearest to the edge of legality. So it is not certain that the policy maker will be prepared to conduct such an action, even if, with the same quantity of goods to be shipped, one might assume that the disappearance of a few businesses would not result in short-term unemployment. We will return to this issue in the section focusing on implementation.

But the important thing here is that the reasoning employed has distanced us from the linear vision and made it possible to use, *to the profit of change*, all the resources offered by the system's complexity. For this complexity is only a handicap if one does not have the intellectual tools, the methods of reasoning, which help to master it and to draw advantage from it. It is then that complexity becomes frightening and leads to inaction, to non-control of action, or to symbolic action – made up of a mixture of sabre rattling and ineffective penalties. To the contrary, knowledge and acceptance of complexity open up unsuspected margins of play. These make it possible to glimpse a variety of opportunities and above all avoid focusing exclusively on the visible part of the iceberg, in other words, on the symptoms.

This is what we can check again with the transport company, that we are using as 'guiding thread' and which we introduced in Chapter 2. Thanks to this case study, we will see not only that using levers can consist of also giving *resources* to actors and not just constraints, but also that the variety of possibilities offered by complex organisations can prove to be both useful in practical terms and enjoyable in intellectual terms.

LINEARITY OF REASONING AND COMPLEXITY OF ORGANISATIONS

We can remember the major symptom worrying the company's managers – agents in direct contact with customers have a recurrent tendency to flee from them, as soon as they find themselves in an awkward situation, although their mission is precisely to provide information and even solutions to travellers in difficulty, and to reassure them if necessary. Higher management gives individual and psychologising explanations to this behaviour of flight: the great majority of agents are assumed to be lazy, unmotivated, interested only in their personal lives to the detriment of any professional investment, even at a low level. The action of change should consequently focus directly on them, and should aim to change their 'attitudes', as if, as we have already said, the relations that they have with customers were taking place outside of all context, in an empty universe, which would leave them totally free to adopt whatever attitude they choose.

Management therefore acts by incantation, since coercion is revealed to be impossible bearing in mind the power held by the unions which, by definition, would immediately oppose it. Now, since general management is itself appraised by the regulatory authorities on the frequency of labour disputes, as all the other actors have known for a long time, it is totally imprisoned by powerful and determined unions, with whom it 'plays' in priority, whom it thinks of as its exclusive contacts, for the reason that they are decision-makers in the event of labour troubles. Paradoxically, this implicit alliance excludes all other actors, in particular the agents themselves, thus producing the remarkable vicious circle which so characterises this company: the more management is afraid of the 'social' context – the unions – the more ready it is to satisfy claims made by these organisations,

and the less capable it is to listen to the real working problems of the
agents who, because of this, become ever more frustrated and demanding,
thus encouraging union activism. In-depth analysis of this situation has
made it possible to highlight two points which will be useful when reasoning on the introduction of real changes in this business.

The Weakness of Middle Management

In the company, middle management is almost totally stripped of power in
the face of the agents that it is supposed to manage. With the notable
exception of what is happening on the ticket sales platforms on departure,
where managers represent a real resource for the sellers, to the extent that
they are capable of both opening extra counters in the case of too much
pressure from customers and, even more important, of repairing an issuing
machine in the case of breakdown, something that is crucial at peak times,
other supervisors or managers control nothing and contribute nothing.
They are not in the transport vehicles with the inspectors in the case of
incidents and they are neither able to provide them with the information
they need nor even to influence decisions that will be taken in terms of
choice between punctuality and connection, which as we have seen are
essential in the face-to-face management between inspectors and travellers.

The Ravages of Verticalisation

More generally, in this business, the agents at the end of the chain have
no organisational resource to accomplish the mission which is officially
assigned to them in the management of customer relations and where they
are reminded, day after day, of the decisive importance of this for a business which is developing in an increasingly competitive world. Because of
the extreme segmentation that is rife in the company, nobody makes the
link between a decision made in one 'pipeline' and its incidence on actors
located elsewhere, and therefore not directly concerned: we have already
seen that the verticalisation of organisations renders any systemic vision
virtually impossible. The consequence of this method of functioning is
that actors have the strong feeling of being laughed at, in the most literal
sense of the term, meaning that they are asked to do something difficult
without ever being concerned about feasibility and, therefore, reality. The
systemic effect resulting from this is that, for these agents, the only
resource available to them is the union organisations that they follow, not
because they are more aware of their situation, but in some sort of a way
by default, using better material advantages to compensate for the actual

disinterestedness in their professional lives demonstrated by their managers. The three strategies that they develop are therefore very rational: escape, as soon as the situation gets complicated and contains risks of conflict with customers; union demands that are always met and yet continually renewed for material advantages of all kinds; strike action at the slightest opportunity, the expression, not understood by line management, of a request to be really integrated into company life and the decisions that are made there. It is wrong to say that in this company union organisations take up too much space or space that does not belong to them. They occupy the space that has been given to them and indeed this is immense.

MICRO DECISIONS AND DEFINITION OF PRIORITIES

Such analysis of an organisation, with its appearance of enormous complexity, at least makes it possible to use simple terms in formulating what would be a true change – simply for the agents to accept that they must remain with the customers in the event of a difficult situation. This ambition is far from being modest for there is no doubt that it is more difficult to implement it than to draw up a vast action plan that is never applied, or to overhaul the structures, which does not change a great deal in the behaviour of actors. One can fully understand the *priority* such as it has just been defined: for the agents who have to face the travellers, this does not signify a change in attitudes which would only depend on themselves and on their goodwill; it means that the consequent parties in the system have been modified in such a way that a new behaviour has been made possible.

This is no longer a change, it is a revolution which will induce some sizeable effects, showing in particular that it is possible to act differently, that nothing is permanently fixed or paralysed in this company. The dynamics of involvement across the rest of the company will no doubt subsequently provoke other major changes which, little by little, will lead to a fundamental transformation of the whole, measurable by the reactions of the customers, as well as in the change observed in the strategies of the actors.

CROSSED PRIORITIES

There is a *second priority* remaining to be defined: on what category must the first efforts be focused? This question is necessary, for if one were trying to get all the agents to change at the same time and at the same speed, one would certainly come up against obstacles such that the overall action would

be bound to fail. This also sheds new light on the concept of priority. No:
only is it important to identify a key point making it possible to unbalance
the system, but it is also necessary to locate the most profitable category, the
one where change has the value of symbol, of proof, of demonstration in
the eyes of the other actors and in particular the managers, because they are
the most difficult to convince of the possibility of getting things moving.

This approach is what we will be calling the search for *crossed priorities*, to the extent that it means combining a field of action with a category.
In the case that we are looking at, it is the inspectors who must play this
role. They are the ones with by far the greatest visibility in relation to the
public, as well as in relation to their peers. They mark the rhythm, they
start the movements, they are a barometer for the company, those to whom
management lends – in vain – all its attention. Getting them to change
behaviour on a subject as delicate as their tense relations with customers
is, in a way, to reverse the whole of the company's logic.

Achieving this sends us back to the question of levers. There is no point,
as we have already said, in simply trying to convince the actors. In an
equivalent context, that is, in the same system of resources and constraints,
their strategy of flight would remain the same. And, at the same time, the
resources that one might wish to give to them, since this is what they lack,
are in the hands of other actors who, for organisational rather than personal
reasons, have little concern for the situation of the inspectors in front of
customers. As a general rule, it is a multitude of little decisions which are
made on a daily basis and which have an effect on this situation. Returning
to these, changing them or tackling them in a different way is the work of
a management that implies self-effacement and does not involve huge and
visible changes in overall structures or regulations. Such action by means
of 'micro decisions' is already in itself a considerable change of context
for the inspectors.

But, more precisely, the first lever used should be applied to the
controllers, the ones who decide on traffic flow. This would involve obtaining from them the definition of reliable and effectively applied criteria when
the question arises of the final choice between punctuality and transport
connections. One might suppose that if such criteria, if they really exist,
for the moment remain vague, this is because the controllers carefully look
after the areas of autonomy in their work. It will therefore be necessary
to offer them something in exchange, or create a constraint for them that
will give more clarity. It will then be up to the company to define a framework within which the choice will be made and possibly a system of positive or negative sanctions attached to its implementation. This definition
will make it possible to return to the inspectors and set up an agreement

with them which could be formulated along the following somewhat colourful lines:

> We, the management, have listened to you and taken a look at your reality. We have understood that if you leave the transport system in a difficult situation, this is not because of lack of interest or professionalism; it is because our method of functioning does not permit you to stay. If we undertake to obtain from the controllers that they base their decisions on criteria that are reliable and known to you and if we penalise the non-application of such criteria, if in addition we make it our business to ensure that the machine maintenance service reads and takes account of your reports on incidents, assuming that you effectively write and communicate these, are you prepared to commit yourselves to managing the relationship with customers when a problem occurs?

This formulation helps to explain that the change is not imposed, that it is not a mechanical effect of the levers used. It is negotiated with the actors, not by speaking to them of moral, general or abstract principles on public service, but by starting out from their own daily reality. In relation to this, it is proposed to give them the resources that will make a change of strategy acceptable – rational – for them. At the same time, we have seen that granting such resources will depend on other actors, whom it will not be any easier to budge. Here again, it will be necessary to use levers, some of which have been mentioned. Nothing is simple, in point of fact.

FROM CLOSE-UP CONTROL TO CONDUCTING THE ORCHESTRA

However, whoever says negotiated agreement also says responsibility. The interesting aspect of what is suggested here is not simply change the strategy of the inspectors, it is also giving them responsibility, making it possible to introduce systems for assessing what they do – something that was impossible to implement while the organisation was unable to provide them with the slightest resource.

One can clearly see the 'avalanche effect' of change that is produced by the use of levers: local management finds itself equipped *de facto* with new resources with which to face the inspectors, as guarantors of the effective use of the criteria that have been defined. It will be able, little by little, to reset the stage, get away from behaviours of withdrawal and return to the place that the previous method of functioning did not allow them to occupy. In counter point, action by the union organisations will be changed by this. Not only will they no longer be in the situation of being the only resources and the only interlocutors for the inspectors, but they will also need to make an effort in parallel with management in order to adhere to the professional realities of their principals and steer away from ideological or terrorist statements.

In such a case and due to what we have called *banding effects* which are inseparable from the use of levers, the proposed change is no longer solely a change in the behaviour of the actors; it is a fundamental evolution of the company's dominant practices – the culture as management writings might say – which, if it occurs, will open up new possibilities, will reveal opportunities, will make it possible to continue the movement far more effectively than an absolute, rigid and long-term planning of the overall process. This will no doubt be less secure in appearance, to the extent that experience shows that it is pointless to try and predict all the consequences induced by the use of levers.

We have over-emphasised the extreme intelligence of the actors to think that all their reactions, all the new arrangements that they will not fail to find, are predictable. And it is indeed they who reveal the new *solutions that are acceptable* while the role of management in this scenario is closer to the orchestra conductor than to the finicky controller watching that things progress in accordance with a predetermined plan.

5 Implementation: The Moment of Change

Having access to a good problematic on change and a solid methodology for analysing organisations is one thing. Implementing change is quite another, and far from easy, as all those interested in the question have been able to see, whether observers or practitioners. On all sides, there is great reticence to accept to 'launching' oneself into the process, which no doubt explains the amount of time and energy spent on drawing up plans which are endlessly being written and are never finally applied. In terms of change more than anything else, the best is the enemy of the good and finicky perfectionism is a powerful factor of immobilism. As everybody shares the same fears at the moment of undertaking something, it is often enough to show managers that all is not ready, that the different steps are neither clear nor under control, that one is not guaranteed the agreement and support of such and such a category, for everything to be blocked and transformations to be adjourned *sine die*.

THE PRINCIPAL FACTORS OF IMMOBILISM

In some organisations, this pressure towards conservatism is aggravated by the turnover of managers which means that none of them is interested in taking the slightest risk, during their short stay at the head of the company, which is part of a career path that must not be marred by any incident. In such situations, change becomes something which everybody is more ready to talk about than do anything about. It is the organisation which is made use of to the profit of those who manage it and not those who serve it, and change is even more likely to become a dominant rhetoric where it is not actually practised.

This is summarised well by Charles Noble when he writes: 'Implementation is not a very popular topic with many managers. Senior executives often invest in week-long retreats, extensive marketing research, and expensive outside consulting services, trying to develop the strategic plans that will lead their companies to a prosperous future. Too often, though, these plans never come to fruition – the expected results fail to materialize.'[1]

To this should be added that what we are talking about here is not so much defining a strategy for the company, but putting organisations in place: that is, methods of functioning, which will lead to their implementation and possibly their success. The difficult is only greater, since in reminding us that the methods of functioning are above all what people do, the way they work, decide, collaborate and sometimes protect themselves, we will at the same time have been reminded of the extent of the issue.[2]

This reticence with regard to implementation and its difficulty is understandable, but it generates a paradox just as management likes them. It is understandable to the extent that, for all the reasons given up until now, this constitutes the most delicate and often the most hazardous part of the change process. We have known for a long time that we have few difficulties in drawing up plans and strategies, even if a good number of these stay in desk drawers or simply end up as dead letters: drawing up detailed programmes is a favourite exercise for immobile organisations, as we have already seen. Even decision-making, although often dangerous, does not constitute an insurmountable obstacle, if the responsibilities are sufficiently diluted in complex discussions aimed at reaching the famous 'consensus', in other words finally taking everybody on board the same boat. But as soon as it involves taking official action. 'deploying' it, that is quite another matter. Why?

TALK OF GOOD SENSE IS NOT NECESSARILY TALK WITH GOOD SENSE

Observation of the mechanisms at work in organisations in general, and in companies in particular, shows that decisions for change are most often taken in accordance with a logic of 'good reason', the one appealing to an actor's good sense in order to be understood: bearing in mind the existing situation, there are good reasons for doing this. But that 'good reason', however evident, however legitimate it may appear, can be likened to the good old 'one best way' of Taylorism: because it is, or is assumed to be, the only way, a decision made must be imposed on all, without possibility of discussion. Questioning it, criticising it, even fighting it can only be the result of incomprehension at best, intellectual dishonesty and bad faith at worst, and in this respect is a matter for reprobation to start with and then sanctions to follow. Implementation, from this point of view, is therefore nothing more than a simple problem of routine management not really worthy of much interest.

Reality is quite different, even if plenty of 'deciders' pretend to ignore it in the name of a theoretical 'general interest': any decision for change has a greater or lesser impact directly on a human system and the strategies of the actors who are in it. We should remember that such strategies represent the intelligent solutions that these actors have found to gain the most advantage from the context in which they have been placed. This is the yardstick they will use to assess, implicitly or explicitly, the decision taken and not its managerial legitimacy. It is a simple 'cost–advantage' calculation that will be made and that will determine the acceptance or refusal, by the actors concerned, of decisions which are taken. *And it is against this calculation that implementation will find itself pitched.* So it is understandable that the more this phenomenon can be anticipated – it is investment in knowledge, listening, so often mentioned already in this book, which permits such anticipation – the more the strategy of implementation can be adapted to this reality.

However, it is precisely the primacy given to the programme – to what it *must* do – as opposed to the knowledge of reality – what it *can possibly* do – that prevents one from anticipating the reactions of the actors. It is here that we find the paradox: since the capacity of any system to refuse what is proposed to it is, at best, under-estimated and, more generally, ignored, its implementation is sub-contracted by the managers to their subordinates, who are left to define the technical procedures that will give concrete expression to the decisions taken. In fact, the subordinates in question are going to have to face up to difficulties far superior to those that their bosses had to deal with when making the decisions in the first place. They are bound to come up against the strategic interests of those involved, against their capacity to oppose, to bend the rules. They will need to come to terms with the different stakeholders and indeed start again from scratch, sometimes including even the decision process itself, where necessary, this time round, involving actors who have until now been ignored – a situation which will not fail, in return, to have profound effects on the content of such decisions.

It is striking to note, in the multitude of cases of this type that we have had to study, to what extent, once the decision has been taken, the bosses stand well back as if implementation were no concern of theirs. Or rather as if, because they themselves have done their work and done it well since the decision taken is technically sound, any difficulty in its application can only come from the clumsiness of those who are in charge of applying it or from the bad faith of those on whom it is applied. The manager becomes the Pontius Pilate of the process of change and cannot really help it if Jesus ends up on the cross! In other words, he has the easy choice, while others have the thankless task of reconciling the desirable with the possible – even if it is always desirable but not always possible to do so.

THE EXAMPLE OF INSURANCE COMPANIES

The effect of this paradox can sometimes be encouraging, as, for example, when we see some junior managers, most often fairly young, thrown into an assignment thought to be of little prestige, and who suddenly find themselves in a situation where they must manage interests which are of course beyond them but which are also beyond their bosses. This is what has happened in a good number of insurance companies: traditionally, insurers have always sub-contracted the relationship with their end customers to intermediaries of various kinds, whether agents, brokers or even salaried sales staff who, although members of the companies in question, were quick to gain their independence. As a consequence of this choice, the companies became extremely dependant on such intermediaries, including when this involved launching new products which they believed to be of undisputable interest for the survival of the whole. In the United States, for example, the leader on the domestic market for general insurance had the utmost difficulty in getting its agents, even though exclusive, to enter the life assurance market.

Because competition was becoming increasingly fierce in this sector as in others, it therefore seemed crucial for the companies to restore contact with the end customer so as to have a better command of the impact of their communications and a closer control over the application of their product or pricing policies. To do this, they wanted to use computerised and electronic tools, suggesting the centralisation of all information available on customers or the systematic collection of all electronic addresses for such customers. The implementation of this, as one might have guessed, was only expected to produce technical problems which helps to explain why, in most cases, it was entrusted to computer departments!

All, as far as we know without exception, had enormous difficulties in applying these new orientations and some never succeeded at all. Naïvely, they explained to their intermediaries that such arrangements would improve and facilitate their own work – so even less reason to oppose them! However the managers of the computer departments in charge of such projects progressively discovered the amplitude of the problems that they were coming up against and that neither themselves nor those making the decisions had anticipated. To their surprise, they discovered that the monopoly of access to the customer was, for the agents, brokers and other salaried sales staff, a priceless resource which guaranteed to them a certain level of power, autonomy and remuneration. And, all things being equal, agreeing to give this up, no matter how good the reason, amounted for them to professional suicide in the true sense of the term, to the extent that, in the long term, they easily anticipated that some of them were certain to disappear, with the companies reabsorbing part of their current work. Faced with such difficulties, the managers in charge of implementation generally called in outside consultants, who often only reinforced the technical orientation of decisions that had been taken, to the detriment of a strategic understanding of the real issues. The development of a 'good information system' has once again taken the place of effectively listening to the actors concerned. The general disorder thus grew bigger, the problem became even more conflictual, until certain managers finally gave up on their project, waiting for better days, which did not necessarily arrive.

THE INERTIA OF ORGANISATIONS

The organisations therefore naturally manifest a huge inertia, which is not specifically linked to their size. In this matter, having to manage a 'human sized' unit is not the guarantee that it will be easier to produce movement, rather the contrary. Pressures towards change will only be more reduced and the reproduction of previous practices will become the rule.

In the case study which he has devoted to two companies – Laura Ashley and Firestone – Donald N. Sull shows with great relevance how immobilism in organisations is constructed and theorised. After noting that 'the problem is not an inability to take action but an inability to take the appropriate action', he analyses what he calls the 'active inertia' which runs rife in companies and which is an enlightening demonstration of the abstract nature of managerial vocabulary, as well as its frequent use as a screen for inaction, in a logic identical to the one we have identified around 'action plans'. Thus, in Sull's opinion, strategic plans lead to blindness, processes are transformed into routines, relationships end up as obstacles and values become dogmas. And he concludes: 'established processes often take on a life of their own. They cease to be a means to an end and become an end in themselves. People follow processes not because they're effective or efficient but because they are well known and comfortable.'[3]

The word 'comfortable' must not be used lightly, in the simple sense of feeling right somewhere or having characteristics which make life easier. Whatever their objectives and ambitions in relation to customers, markets or the general public, whatever their 'project' and the 'vision' of their executives which underlie them, organisations have a natural tendency over time to privilege their internal logic over their mission, which constitutes the principal source of inertia, and explains why managers feel the need to theorise this unmentionable practice.

The theory, with its accompanying vocabulary, is what will explain, justify or cover over the ever growing distance between declared intentions and effective behaviours. The more an organisation falls into routine, privileges the repetition of well-known and well-mastered solutions, the more, in reality, it will only function to protect its members to the detriment of any other consideration such as service quality or cost reductions. At the same time, it is going to adopt a modernist or technocratic vocabulary corresponding to current trends, together with superficial practices assumed to represent or symbolise profound changes – use first names in the American style, ostensibly leave one's door open, mix with other job categories in the staff canteen, and so on. But as soon as this puts 'comfort' in jeopardy, things become far more difficult and resistances more numerous and more open. They come from all around.

THE VICIOUS CIRCLE OF CONSERVATISM

Among managers, there are those for whom it is never the right moment and who endlessly put off until tomorrow what they should be doing today. How often does one hear senior managers delivering, with surprising detachment, a brilliant analysis, usually very relevant, of what is not right in their organisation, pointing the finger at all that should be changed, defining with lucidity what the final result should be, at the same time as emphasising in apology that 'now is not the time' and that 'people' – the others, of course – 'are not ready'. It is a constant in a lot of organisations to observe this vicious circle of immobility: on one side, the managers would like to change, at least in appearance, but consider that their troops are not ready to follow them along this road; and on the other side, the troops in question do not see why they should make a move when those in charge show such immobility. Most specialists however are in agreement in recognising that it is at the top that the essentials of the problem are to be found.

In this way, Hammer and Stanton write as follows on the specific case of setting up a process organisation:

> Because the changes involved in becoming a process enterprise are so great, companies can expect to encounter considerable organizational

resistance. We have found, though, that it's rarely the frontline workers who impede the transformation. Once they see that their jobs will become broader and more interesting, they are generally eager to get on board. Rather, the biggest source of resistance is usually senior functional executives, division heads, and other members of the top management team. These senior executives will often either resent what they see as a loss of autonomy and power or be uncomfortable with the new, collaborative managerial style.[4]

The observation is shrewd and can easily be generalised to cover all situations of change. It also shows that 'comfort' and its defence form an obstacle that is evenly distributed across all categories of an organisation and are not simply created by 'people'.

THE DEFENCE OF WHOSE ASSETS?

The intermediary organs of representation – the union organisations – are to a greater or lesser degree in the same situation, the only significant difference being that they are not in charge of the company's management, or responsible for preparing it to face up to the future. However, the behaviour that they develop is the same since their logic is the same. Involved in the actual functioning, having for the most part adopted the segmented structures of their members along the same lines as the organisation in which they are implanted, they perceive any tendency towards change as a threat. When they focus on the 'defence of assets', the expression used can be understood at two levels. These are the assets of their principals, certainly, the conquest of which is always amplified and idealised by a warlike vocabulary, but they are also and maybe above all their own, their structures, their practices, their jobs, their routines.

This situation leads to many blockages which, as we will see, are all the more difficult to overcome when the 'weight of welfare' is heavy in an organisation. This is what we have already seen in the transport company case in which the union organisations become the privileged, even exclusive, contacts for a general management that is paralysed by the fear of social organisations. In order to avoid strikes and other demonstrations of discontents by its partners, management satisfies claims that are always more numerous and sometimes farfetched, but which are in fact those of the union organisations themselves, and so always oriented towards conservatism and reinforcement of the existing order. Of course, as in the case of the management, such conservatism conceals itself under a progressive vocabulary, vaunting service to the customer, the public, the citizen or the student.

It is also probable that such union conservatism is behind the impressive fall in the membership rates that today characterises all developed countries, with the sole exception of Sweden. In France, the rate of unionisation fell between 1985 and 1995 from 14.5 per cent to 9.1 per cent, an absolute record. Over the same period in the United States, it fell from 18.1 per cent to 14.2 per cent. And what can we say about New Zealand where, over the same time, it dropped from 54.1 per cent to 24.3 per cent?[5] Behind this phenomenon there is not just a general disinterest in the common weal. When employees want to defend themselves, they spontaneously find their own forms of organisation as was shown by the eruption of 'coordinations' in France. It is the unsuitability of the methods of functioning for taking new problems into account which is at cause. At the start of the year 2000 France provided a particularly striking example of immobility linked to the strict defence of established union positions.

While, for obvious reasons of improving the service to the taxpayer and reducing the cost of this service,[6] the French Minister of Economy and Finance was trying to merge or at least bring closer the two main administration services of this Ministry – the General Tax Division and Public Accounting – the unions were violently opposed to the project. They mobilised employees and local councillors for the motive that this measure was a threat to employment and involved closing down local administrative units, thus complicating the lives of users and local parish councillors. The official denials, even though in good faith and with proof to support them, were of no help. It was necessary to withdraw the reform and the Minister was forced pitifully to present a resignation that was rapidly accepted. And yet most of the observers were in agreement on one point. The real issue of the battle was a reappraisal of the balance between the two main union organisations in this Ministry. One was particularly established in one administration, the other in the second, and a tacit agreement allowed them to benefit from this situation without seeking to compete against each other. The planned merger which, in effect, resulted in the absorption of part of one of the administrations concerned by the second, would have had major consequences on the balance between the unions. However well-founded the foundation for the decision, it was unacceptable by definition.

AND WHAT ABOUT THE EMPLOYEES?

There is nothing to say, finally, that change is spontaneously more acceptable by the employees themselves. This is a 'basist' naïvety which must be corrected. The organisational changes proposed at the dawn of the twenty-first century are indeed those of *work*, the ways of doing it, including relationships that one has with others in the businesses. However work, in contemporary companies, has always had two functions: a production function – producing goods and services to put on the market – and a protection function – protecting those who work not only from the hazards of life by providing them with the means of subsistence, but also from others, such as customers and colleagues.[7] What we can see today, what is in fact targeted by most organisational changes, is the end of the work protection function. The 'duty of cooperation' which is imposed on everybody, with all that implies in the way of negotiation, confrontation, dependency and discomfort in work,[8] is one of the most significant aspects of this. Actors anticipate it with too much difficulty, and their intelligence allows them to understand and to catch sight of the concrete consequences of what they are being asked for. They are required to abandon a great deal without necessarily being offered a reasonable alternative.

This situation shows itself to be even more delicate if the organisation concerned is bureaucratic in nature; that is, turned in on itself and its members.[9] In such a case, it is not the legitimacy of change that will pose the problem. All serious investigations show that employees, even those in the most immobile of organisations, understand that work can no longer be what it was, which does not prevent them from regretting it; what will be the determining factor here is the implementation – the way in which the problem is shared with them and in which they are associated with the search for solutions.[10]

CHANGE IN LITTLE STEPS

The consequence of what has just been said is that change, in organisations, has two major features. In the majority of cases this is not voluntarist, in the sense that it is not the result of a decision to change made by a responsible actor. It arrives of its own volition, following on from spontaneous developments or small decisions which, when put end to end, lead to something new and often unexpected. Change happens without people noticing, and the 'leader's' role is therefore not so much to be in front, thanks to his 'vision', as to follow behind and, if he can, to accompany, and in any case not to hinder. Then, one day, one realises with amazement that things are no longer what they were. The external context changes, decisions are taken in a field which profoundly affects another field, thus creating a natural process of which one does not speak simply because one does not see it. This is the way in which the great majority of organisations have succeeded in adapting themselves. It is also the fault of this process that others have died. Spontaneous change is, above all, the reign of the random, of surprises that may be good as well as bad.

But that means that *the change being looked for is a phenomenon that is far more reactive than proactive*. It is a response and not an anticipation, as shown by that sports adage which states that one should not change a winning team. One must wait to lose before reacting, and experiences of change from cold – although they do exist – can be counted on one's fingers.

From a certain point of view, there is nothing surprising in that Changing something that is going well is simply not legitimate in the eyes of the actors concerned. Although one can get them to understand and really grasp the necessity when things go badly, they will nevertheless feel frustration in having to change things that are going well, and will not fail to put those playing God on guard. Rarely will you see healthy people sitting in doctors' waiting rooms. In terms of organisation, prevention is a cause which still remains to be pleaded. However, finding the 'right moment for change' poses the problem of legitimacy for action, that the hierarchical position is even less capable of dealing with when the stakes are high in terms of power or comfort for those concerned. Everybody knows today that it is a crisis situation that confers such legitimacy, sometimes modestly called 'learning the lesson from a failure'. The true lesson should be that one must not wait for the crisis.

WHY CHANGE WHEN EVERYTHING IS GOING WELL?

We have been able to observe a situation of this type: a European business is producing a 'commodity' that it distributes either directly to its biggest customers or by means of a network of independent dealers who serve the general public. It is the world leader in its market, very well established in North America, where it is performing remarkably well. Its President, who is a benchmark in the business, enjoys an excellent image outside and an undeniable charisma with managers and employees inside the company. Management is sound and the stock market price translates the very positive evaluation of the financial markets. The organisation is uniform, wherever in the world operations are being run, and has recently been modified to give better satisfaction to customer expectations: regional structures have been put in place, within which teams of technical sales engineers maintain direct and fast-moving relationships with customers, so as to satisfy any new requirements within the shortest possible time. The principle is simple: the requirement of proximity in relation to customers involves the fullest possible decentralisation of operations, and freedom for people in the 'field' to decide how they want to manage their relations with their environment.

Such re-organisation did not pose any problems and the financial results continued to be remarkable. And yet the President expressed a doubt on its real effectiveness, more linked to personal intuition than to the deterioration of any particular indicator. He had a survey carried out in several countries in order to have a better understanding of how the company really functioned and the way in which local actors had assimilated the new set-up. Research showed that his intuition was correct and that the decentralisation was producing an unexpected effect likely to be damaging over time to the relationship with customers who, seizing the opportunity offered to them to address easily contactable local representatives, did not hesitate to transmit to them all their demands, which were of course proving to be far more numerous than anticipated.

Faced with such an influx, the technical sales engineers moved as quickly as they could. They gave priority treatment to the easiest questions, those that were within their field of competence, and put off until later those that required an investment in terms of searching for new solutions. Their over-work allowed them to justify the choices they made, without management, itself snowed under with work, having sufficient distance to appreciate the reality of the situation and maybe correct it. The customers did not take long to understand that, if they had a question that was the slightest bit complex in content, requiring innovation, it was better to turn towards a competitor eager to win new market share from the world leader which, in this way, became the champion of routine, while its competitors, thanks to market demand, went several lengths ahead in terms of technological innovation. The market, however, was buoyant enough for this phenomenon, still only at its beginnings, not to show in the financial figures.

Nevertheless, seeing the results of the survey, which confirmed his intuitions, the President decided to correct the line of fire and changed his organisation once again in order to make it more responsive. Among the actions put forward was, in particular, a significant change in the methods of appraisal and remuneration for engineers together with the overall line management chain. This measure was intended to correct the quantitative drift induced by the abundance of requests, and to place everybody in the position of having to arbitrate between replies that were easy and those requiring research and inventiveness.

The change met with failure; not because the results were not good. It was simply not put in place subsequent to a generalised opposition in particular from upper management which did not see the need for changing something that, despite what the President had to say, ensured the company's success. Everybody found themselves in agreement in emphasising the risks that would be incurred by stirring up the opposition of the engineers, from whom so much was already required, and managers in the different countries voiced their doubts on the wisdom of changing yet again something that had only just been put in place. It was a true action of lobbying which took place, backed by scarcely veiled threats, until the President cancelled his project – to everybody's great relief.

THE WINDOWS OF OPPORTUNITY

One might conclude from this that change does not happen when it is necessary, *but when it is possible.* It is the appearance of this *window of opportunity*, to use military parlance, that is known as the *moment of change.* This moment is, by definition, difficult to identify since it does not obey any specific rule which might be theorised by means of a reliable model. It comes from an alchemy which must be felt rather than demonstrated and which doubtless corresponds to the meeting point between a situation which is undeniably deteriorating and therefore known to everybody, and the feeling shared by a majority of actors that things cannot and will not continue as before.

It is for this reason that certain crises, even major ones, are not enough to make change possible. If these are seen only in a deterioration of results that do not really put the organisation in danger, if they are only expressed by a poorer service rendered to customers who, in any case, do not have much choice, and, lastly, if they concern units whose members enjoy protection such that they would need a lot more to make them aware of the catastrophe, then there is little chance of them triggering any reaction at all.

In such characteristics, one can recognise the French national education system which everybody agrees year after year is totally against any shape of reform, even though the results that it produces are in inverse proportion to the resources that it consumes. This world is so turned in on itself, with advantages of every kind, not the least of which is for a high proportion of its members not to find themselves in front of pupils, that any change is, *de facto*, a threat to such advantages. The environment can shift to a point where it will become inevitable to make a fundamental change in the organisation, concerning not only the training of teachers, the disciplines that they teach, but also the modalities in accordance with which they are appraised and remunerated, as well as the way in which they perform their jobs.

But nothing happens, it is never the right moment. One can see that the pupils are different, more difficult, more demanding, but this is only a matter for regret, not for adaptation.

The transport company shows almost exactly the same characteristics and helps us to understand how executives can *miss* the moment of change. Faced with a worsening service that leads high contribution customers to turn towards other means of transport as soon as they possibly can, management continues imperturbably with its odd face-to-face with the union organisations, for reasons already mentioned above. These, as we have said, function in accordance with their own special logic, conservative by definition, and in this case immobilist. Both partners are in agreement on the necessity to do nothing that would threaten the delicate balances, thereby increasing the disinvestment of groups who get the feeling that nobody is concerned about them.

But all the surveys that were carried out have shown, on the one hand, worsening work situations, to which actors only accommodate themselves by reducing the constraints, that is, by doing less and less work, and, on the other hand, a certain readiness to try to 'do things differently' provided one is capable of discussing with them alternatives that concern their everyday reality and not simply the deformed and biased perception that institutional partners have of them. Paradoxically, as already seen in other companies, it will most probably be through a major crisis *provoked by the agents themselves* that the opportunity will arise for fundamentally changing this organisation. From this point of view, the Air France case study, which will be presented in the next chapter, is a classic of its kind. It was necessary for the employees to take action, occupy runways, workshops and offices in order to get something decided, simply because it was no longer possible to carry on doing nothing.

LISTENING AND THE MOMENT OF CHANGE

So one can fully understand the necessity for *listening* in order to identify the moment of change. This must be aimed first at the actors themselves and not those who represent them, whom as we have already said have an apprehension of reality that is distorted by their own interests. This is not a case of short-circuiting or anti-unionism. The unions, like other actors, must be put in a situation in which they will have an *interest* in doing their work. This will occur if, when faced with their assertions and demands presented in the name of their members, a management is capable of putting forward an understanding of reality gained in the field and constructed on a true analysis of working situations. It is this *true reality* which may constitute a real opportunity to do something with the backing of the actors and not by directly confronting their opposition which is more assumed than real.

Experience shows that listening, which is what we are talking about here, is made easier when an event occurs, whether this is a failure, a major crisis or any other shock striking the organisation. In such circumstances, the actors talk, communicate their personal understanding of events, *which is always interpretable from their own situation*. A failure will, in most cases, allow the person speaking to say not what is not right in general, *but what is not right for him*. The event in question will be quickly forgotten in the conversation to make way for an open discussion on what the actor himself feels is intolerable or needs to be changed.

In other words, the actors will use what is happening as an unexpected resource for expressing something that until then they had only felt in a confused way, or that the ambient conformism virtually prevented them from admitting to themselves. One of the great virtues of crises, is to make the inexpressible expressible and allow individuals to realise that they are all thinking alike without ever having dared talk of it to each other.

A FAILED MERGER: A FORMIDABLE MEANS OF REVEALING AN ORGANISATION'S UNDERLYING PROBLEMS

This is what happened in a big bank in Northern Europe at the beginning of 2000. The presentation of this case will help to highlight some facets of the opportunities that appear when an unexpected event occurs and loosens the tongues of the actors concerned, even if caution suggests, once again, that it should be used only as an example and not as a model.

A financial establishment on the European marketplace has a solid reputation for serious and sound management, built up over time by Presidents coming from the Civil Service. And yet the caution of such management has not prevented it from expanding outside the national territory, particularly with regard to all investment bank activities. To do this, the bank has proceeded with well targeted purchases, mostly in North America, which show it to be an influential operator on world financial markets.

Culturally speaking, the dominant feature in this organisation is a high level of conformism, somewhat 'stuffy' relations and a rebuttal of interpersonal conflicts, which continually pushes towards a search for consensual solutions, even if this means delaying the decision-making process.

Traditionally, one waits for things to be 'ripe' before launching oneself into action – for them to have been accepted before being officially decided. In appearance, the social climate is excellent, supported by good levels of pay, attractive career possibilities, and not insignificant advantages, acknowledged by the employees.

Like a good number of its sister banks, this bank was sucked into the whirlpool of mergers and acquisitions towards the end of the 1990s. This pushed it into reviewing its strategy which, until then, had been more inclined to privilege alliances over marriages – jealous as it was of its independence and its specificities. So as not to remain outside the big concentrations, the directors chose to launch a friendly takeover bid for one of the major business banks on the marketplace, known and respected worldwide for more than a century.

The transaction was launched in all transparency and with full agreement between the two executive teams. Task forces were quickly set up, even before the markets had given their verdict. These teams combined managers from both establishments, happy to work together on forming an overall structure with more weight. As always in such circumstances, a few frictions were revealed around some perfectly understandable susceptibilities, although actors were in agreement in saying that, here, there were real opportunities for discovering new things.

But the story comes to a sudden stop with the arrival of a third establishment, itself a big and generalist rival of the first, which launched a hostile takeover bid for both banks which had already gone a long way in their merger process. After various incidents, causing the whole country to hold its breath through that summer, the affair sorted itself out in a surprising way – the first bank managed to slip out of its predator's clutches, while the investment bank, although not its principal prey, remained trapped.

The managers and employees followed events on a day-to-day basis, especially those from the investment bank side, primarily concerned by the initial merger project. A defence association was set up and management appealed to the patriotism of its employees, calling on them to refuse to hand over their own shares to the hostile competitor. There were no defections, which helps to explain the President's feeling of huge success with the final outcome – the bank saved its independence – which he hastened to share with all the head office managers, using an improvised general meeting held in the bank's main lobby to tell them the details of the final negotiation.

Curiously, this presentation was poorly received, generating an unpleasant atmosphere, and a huge gap appeared between top management, who saw the event as a victory, and management staff who appeared sullen with this end to the adventure. Without actually spelling it out, the service provided by top management was criticised, and they were reproached for only having lived the event from their own point of view and not having 'felt' how the employees were living it.

This persistent malaise was to lead the person in charge of the investment bank side, by definition the most affected by this epic, to start up a survey with his managers for 'listening' – this is the term used – to them in order to understand how they themselves have experienced this period of time. The method used would help to understand reactions, not from an emotional point of view, but by putting them in context with the organisation's method of functioning. This is what we have already defined as listening which, we must remember, does not consist solely of asking people what they want or why they are not happy, but also telling them.

The results were surprising: the merger's failure – for this in fact was how managers had seen the events – was, amazingly, to loosen tongues in this usually tight-lipped environment. Senior management was to be brutally and unreservedly exposed to question, almost as if the task force teams set up to prepare the finally abortive merger had formed a sort of external audit revealing all the bank's weaknesses – organisational as well as strategic. Everything took place as though the merger had represented, in the collective unconscious, a non-dramatic and official way of resolving these problems.

All this is clearly understood from a certain number of paradoxes encountered during interview sessions conducted with the managers. In this way, although they showed themselves extremely critical of their organisation, which they reproached pell-mell for its lack of strategic vision, a terrible weight of bureaucratic red tape which seemed to grow and flourish, an absence of coherence in decision-making, an archaic and relatively unprofessional management, methods of promotion only poorly linked to real performances, and so on, in parallel, each person individually appeared content with their lot, with their work that was generally thought to be interesting, with their remuneration that was considered generous, or with the many opportunities that were offered to them.

Along the same lines, human resource management was subjected to acerbic criticism with regard to the lack of serious career management for managers, to systems of remuneration that were distant from the reality of work and the business world, although at the same time everybody was more or less satisfied with their lot and with the proposals for development which were actually made to them. Certain reproaches were focused on actual business practices, in particular risk management, a sensitive subject of great bureaucratic complexity as soon as it involved obtaining authorisation, while others targeted the excessive centralisation and pointless intervention of too many varied and sundry managers, which everybody seemed to put up with in their corner by setting up official networks allowing them, finally without too many problems, to escape from limits and obstacles of all kinds. The organisation's capacity to manage its customers, especially the most important ones, was seriously contested, highlighting the extreme compartmentalisation that was prevalent in the company, the multiplicity of contacts, the continual short-circuiting, without anybody, however, at any particular time having tried to change anything whatsoever, with each person building up their own customer portfolio, managed as autonomously as possible, and only calling on the rest of the establishment with the utmost caution.

INTERPRETATION OF THE MALAISE

Such contradictions – which, like all contradictions, are only apparent – have led to a reappraisal of the bank's real method of functioning, and above all to an understanding of the origins of this vague but clearly identifiable malaise, which meant that this universe, which was seen by everybody as very stable, if not conservative and immobile, was in fact ready for profound changes. The contradictions only existed if one stayed with the official picture of the organisation, seen as homogenous and integrated, which in reality was not the case.

It appeared that, behind the rhetoric of belonging to a single establishment, the company was made up of very independent small or medium-sized units, within which everybody managed to find the necessary arrangements for carrying out their work under satisfactory conditions, with regard to immediate customer care, as well as the creation of opportunities to develop business. Hence, consequently, a strong link with one's own unit which, paradoxically, weakened the general organisation by making it the target for all criticisms, whether justified or not. In their local universe, each person had the possibility of demonstrating talents recognised by their peers, had the feeling that they were 'playing in the first division' and above all had the freedom to build up their own customer portfolio, which increased their value on the job market.

But, at the same time, the company confusedly felt the need to control the centrifugal pulls developed by all these little entities, always tempted by greater autonomy, and content with 'doing their deals' in the services suggested to them by central departments. For this, it was continually strengthening the structures for steering, for coordination and for control: always more meetings, more resource centres, more support functions.

The gap, which never stopped widening between these two areas, allowed each side to use the other as a foil and an alibi: central units considered local brokers to be interested solely in their bonuses and personal futures, while the brokers saw 'head office managers' as being totally cut off from business reality, purely concerned with preserving their positions.

This situation thus led to one of those rather unoriginal vicious circles that are frequently encountered in this type of organisation: the peripheral units were continually seeking to expand their freedom and margins for manoeuvre, thus creating a powerful centrifugal movement which, in the eyes of the central functions, gave them the appearance of an impenetrable world, requiring always more control and organisation. The antagonism between the two sides continued to grow.

The problem was that this method of functioning set limits on global performance in a world in which competition was becoming ever more intense. On one hand, ambitions with regard to customers, themselves becoming more and more global, were reduced to what each unit was capable of offering through its own competence alone, without ever making use of possible synergies; on the other hand, uncontrolled risk management, sometimes over-lax, sometimes over-cautious, left the bank dangerously exposed on the market. And even for the managers living in these small units and liking them, career prospects were seen to be very dependant on the size of such units and their possibilities of growth.

So, ultimately, it was the whole bank's commercial possibilities that were severely penalised by this method of functioning, in precisely the sector on which it focused as a priority. And this 'game', quite possible in a stable situation, suddenly found itself threatened by pressure from competitors, reinforced by that from shareholders to whom considerable promises had been made. In brief, everybody was trapped in a zero sum game where the failure of the merger, which had clearly shown, through the contact with another bank working on the same market niches, that other practices were possible, that considerable developments were in progress at competitors, forced actors to open their eyes. The dissatisfaction that was expressed, the growing frustration and the bitter criticism, sometimes without disguise, of general management could be interpreted as so many signs sent out by the managers who were unanimous in demanding fundamental and rapid changes.

There, where nobody had seen anything but conservatism and conformism, suddenly appeared the *will and the possibility* for more far-reaching change than even the most optimistic among them had dared to contemplate.

THE CHEMISTRY OF CHANGE

This is the moment of change, and this example provides an opportunity to reflect on it. In their initial vision, the senior executives had indeed understood that, at one moment or another, it would be necessary to change the organisation's practices. Previous surveys had in particular shown that their local representatives were finding it increasingly difficult to respond to complex customer expectations. However, up until then, and in order to avoid making any fundamental changes to working methods, which might have caused conflict from a certain number of actors, their response had been 'always more': more central structures, more committees, more coordination functions, which of course led them to wonder about the reasons for the exponential growth of such functions and their cost. Expecting immobility from employees, these senior executives saw the merger as a chance to get things moving, without having to take the risk themselves of initiating the movement *ex nihilo*.

It was in fact the non-merger that produced this effect and opened the window of opportunity, into which everybody rushed, all reproaching one another for their previous immobility. This was the *developer* which enabled this moment to be seen.

The word is used here with its chemical meaning: spread over an apparently blank page, it 'develops' everything that was in reality on the page but that nobody could see, since, without the developer, the page would continue to appear uniformly white. But, at the same time, the appearance of this developer, of what will play this role, is unpredictable. First, because provoking a crisis oneself in order to change an organisation is perhaps possible in theory, but a luxury that nobody can afford to offer themselves. If the crises arrives, it may be profitable, although the cost in human and financial terms is generally substantial, but it can hardly be provoked knowingly.

The example which has just been discussed suggests something different, once again a long way from being a paralysing form of planning: one can be aware of the need to change, and yet also be anxious when it is time to take action, especially, as we might repeat, if nothing in the situation really justifies it. Even better, we have just seen that everybody can be in agreement on this necessity, and yet nobody will say it out loud, for fear of being isolated or out of step. So those who can, the senior executives, create an event – in this case a merger. But what happens then is difficult to predict and control with nothing to indicate that it absolutely must be done. What has been started often provokes unexpected reactions, which must be seen as so many opportunities to be used. In the bank's case, the merit of its senior executives is not in having undertaken a securely hedged process, but rather of having been able to listen, to go beyond the spontaneous discontent and of having used it as a lever. By doing this, *they have turned the constraint into a resource*, which is no doubt the best way of not allowing the moment of change to slip by unnoticed.

This fundamental unpredictability of the moment of change redefines the role of the manager or 'leader' that we have seen shaping itself over the pages. Ultimately, it is not putting everything that will happen under control – or at least attempting to put it under control. Not only is this impossible, as experience has frequently shown but, when one tries too hard, one generally seems to produce blockages, associated with the bureaucratic nature of the formal procedures that everybody strives to put in place in order to cover themselves. This role is far more evident in a continual process of listening, not superficial or biased, which makes it possible to glimpse possibilities a step ahead and use them to advantage.

It means *accompanying* things with the actors themselves, in an atmosphere of trust. The more thorough the listening, the more such trust will be natural and reciprocal. It is managers who *do not know what is going on* who are the principal factors of blockage to change in the organisations of which they are in charge.

USING DISSATISFACTION AS AN OPPORTUNITY

One last point merits our attention: whether speaking of 'window of opportunity' or 'legitimacy' of change, one always refers sooner or later to a crisis situation, a malaise, in any case outside of daily routine, which makes it possible and acceptable to get things moving. In doing this, one rediscovers a paradox that specialists have been emphasising for years – *one does not achieve change with people who are satisfied.* The phenomenon was particularly evident towards the end of the 1970s in banks and insurance companies, when they tried to introduce computers into the management of all their operations and when certain of them tried to reduce the lines of hierarchy. They quickly came up against a lack of enthusiasm or even direct opposition from their most satisfied employees, those who benefited from the previous system, from its opacity with regard to the real content of their work. Certain companies therefore decided to try some experiments, forming groups made up of employees identified as being dissatisfied with their lot, initially perceived as being not very cooperative and not terribly interested in the company's life. The success was immediate, those involved played the game and discovered new ways of functioning that were more open, more in step with what the company wanted to do, and who were subsequently able to make themselves heard by the whole organisation. This was also a way of getting away from those zero sum games which, as we have seen, can be so very paralysing.[11]

In such a case, it is the *opportunity for change* which should be spoken of, rather than the moment of change. Being on the lookout for all the dissatisfactions that manifest themselves in human populations, *and hence the desire for change*, is once again to give oneself the possibility of transforming what is only perceived as a constraint into a resource. Our habitual stubbornness in considering those who are not content, and who say so, as a threat – because by doing that they are implicitly criticising us, because they challenge the established order of things and run the risk of spreading like an oil slick, or simply because they do not agree – prevents us from grasping the opportunity that they represent. Nigel Nicholson says much the same when, after having discussed evolutionary psychology, he asserts: 'despite the excellent press that change is given, almost everyone resists it – except when they are dissatisfied.'[12] It almost goes without saying.

6 Implementation: Playing on Trust

At the end of 1993, Air France, a flag-carrier of long standing and the pride of a whole country, marked by a history made up of daily exploits, literally exploded. Not only was the company producing record losses, the like of which, until then, had never been seen in the business, but the fall in unit revenues was picking up speed dramatically.[1] During the month of November, there started to appear the signs of social unrest which, little by little, spread like an oil stain and rapidly transformed themselves into an occupation without concessions of the runways on the capital's two main airports, thus causing a complete paralysis of traffic. One can measure the extent of the malaise through such actions, because attacking the work tool, particularly over a long period, was not in the traditions of this business. At the same time, the conflicts grew more severe to the point where, in places, they led to physical violence between managers and employees. There was great confusion, the unions were sometimes left behind and, after many tergiversations, the public authorities, giving way to all kinds of pressures, decided to get rid of the company's President who had nonetheless fought tooth and nail to try to save what was saveable. This departure was supposed to cause a shock and thus unblock the situation.

His replacement was quickly appointed. He was not in any way a specialist of the aviation sector. A former French government Prefect who had successfully conducted difficult negotiations in New Caledonia, he had also held the functions of President of the Paris City transport authority (RATP), from which he resigned in a blaze of publicity after a disagreement with his supervisory Minister. He had the reputation of being a free mind, capable of sorting out even the most conflictual of situations. He immediately surrounded himself with a team of loyal supporters which, in a way, 'doubled up' on the existing team, but was not made up of aviation specialists. It appeared as time went by that this character was in fact somewhat of an advantage since it allowed these senior executives to focus an open and unbiased eye on the company and on events.

A TRUE LISTENING PROCESS

The new President immediately attacked the most glaring problems, calling for immediate measures, in such areas as unit revenues or purchasing. Far

95

be it from us to say that his sole preoccupation was carry out a sociological diagnosis which would then allow him to resolve the overall difficulties. Nevertheless, one of his first decisions was to give himself the means of understanding what were the mechanisms at work that explained the simultaneous deterioration in results and social climate, since he sensed that these were both linked. Indeed, everybody had been struck by the lack of understanding that had progressively spread between executives and employees: the former, aware of how serious the situation was, appealed to the company patriotism of employees for them not to complicate this even more with social unrest; the latter had agreed to make real efforts, particularly in terms of productivity, which not only did not result in an improved situation, but also did not prevent management from suggesting a freeze or even a reduction in salaries. It was therefore a matter of urgency to get out of this blockage situation, and the President believed that this was only possible by resuming a dialogue based on *real and unbiased knowledge*.

This was why the decision was made to give one month (including Christmas and New Year!) to a team of sociologists specialising in organisations, in order to carry out a series of one-off and extremely targeted business reviews on the company's supposedly sensitive areas. These covered freight, maintenance, Paris stopovers (Orly and Charles de Gaulle), cockpit and cabin personnel. In total, 105 in-depth interviews were simply carried out with a carefully selected sample of people. The fact that the survey was carried out at all is surprising. While advice of caution was given to those conducting the interviews, while everybody expected the worst difficulties, or even the refusal of agents to reply to questions, the opposite occurred. Not a single refusal and a fairly warm welcome, revealing a strong desire to express themselves. It is true that it had been decided to play the game of transparency: from the very start of the investigation, several interviewees posed the question of how much it was costing, since the previous involvement of a firm of consultants had been the subject of much controversy. The interviewers answered the question openly, thus creating an atmosphere of trust which did not waver. One saw agents arrive for interviews with a piece of paper in their hands on which they had written what their workmates wanted them to ask on their behalf. Intended to last $1\frac{1}{2}$ hours, the interviews, some of which took place at night in the workshops, sometimes lasted as long as three hours,[2] and revealed a wealth of information, expressing much bitterness and a feeling of having been frequently deceived, but also high hopes of seeing things change. This suggests that the next part of the process could and should rely heavily on this goodwill, provided one knew how to use it advisedly.

THE FACTORS OF A GENERALISED LACK OF UNDERSTANDING

The presentation of these results to the management committee was a delicate manoeuvre. Despite the precautions taken by the President and by the consultants making this presentation, these results showed, by means of a series of carefully chosen examples, the gap that had formed between the organisation's theoretical functioning and its actual functioning, as well as the extent to which the latter had ended up escaping from the control of upper management. One characteristic was particularly noticeable, seen in all the sectors being studied – one was in the presence of a universe that was segmented in accordance with a technical logic, continually enforced and reinforced by the requirements of security. This produced a verticality, or bureaucracy, in the sense of the priority always given by the organisation to its own problems, which tended to generate catastrophic vicious circles. On the one hand, this way of working, without any cooperation between people who were attached to different services and logics, badly affected the quality of service rendered to the customer and led to losses of market share, especially in relation to high contribution customers; on the other hand, the same mechanisms increased costs, as seen everywhere, without everybody's goodwill and dedication, which really existed, being able to offset the deficiencies of the overall system. So, for example, remarkable gains in physical productivity had been made to the freight division, in the loading and unloading of aircraft but, because the methods of functioning had remained the same, they resulted in longer time periods and therefore in a less effective service. This was only one case among several, but it helped to explain why the company's performances *and* the social climate deteriorated simultaneously. On one side, the gains in productivity had been achieved in a mechanical and sometimes brutal manner, without paying attention to conditions which made them possible and effective; on the other side, they had resulted in heavy pressure on employees, which had only led to aggravation of the overall and individual situations. Under such conditions, appealing for a new financial effort from the personnel could only lead to all kinds of fantastical interpretations on the identity of those who were appropriating the gains achieved, and the conflicts expressed the message from the organisation to its executives, which could be summed up simply as follows: 'Do it, but do it differently.'

BREAKING THE TRADITIONAL RELATIONSHIP BETWEEN THE ORGANISATION AND ITS EMPLOYEES

Another contradiction was observed, again showing that, although the need for change was clearly evident and although real and in-depth actions had been initiated, the strategy for implementation had been partly neglected. Traditionally, in this business, employees had benefited from good conditions of work and satisfactory wages. Well protected in the more general sense of the term, they had, in return, developed a culture of loyalty and dedication to the company, which was seen, on a daily basis, in the acceptance of the overlapping of schedules, a particular care in work and a concern for the task to be accomplished under optimal conditions. All this did was express the traditional loyalty–protection link that was encountered in this company, as in plenty of others, and to which agents had long been attached, as evidenced in the operational myth which meant that, whatever the difficulties, an aircraft always left on time. But under pressure from competition, the need to control and reduce costs became apparent and resulted, here as elsewhere, in this link being broken, since the company was no longer able to offer its employees the same conditions, the same advantages or even the same protection. When one of the components of this tacit agreement was broken, they responded by breaking the other, which was immediately interpreted by some managers in terms of a loss of motivation, or even as the sign of moving from one generation of employees who were dedicated and competent to a generation of youngsters who had only a moderate involvement in work. Here again, understanding was at its lowest ebb, encouraging biased interpretations, accusations and more radical conflicts.

Such results called for fundamental action on the methods of functioning, but these seemed difficult to undertake in their present state, bearing in mind the degree of distrust that had spread across the company. The president therefore suggested that the results should be presented in strictly identical terms, using the same supporting evidence, to the highest possible number of the company's employees. This was done during a multitude of 'restitution' meetings, held over a very short space of time, which made it possible to discuss with agents the principal characteristics of their organisation and to share with them, little by little, a similar interpretation of the main problems that the company was facing, expressed in organisational terms and thus never casting doubt on the goodwill, involvement or dedication of a professional category. These presentations gave rise to debates, animated but never aggressive, allowing everybody to express their feelings and also giving the sociologists an opportunity to correct and complete certain of their analyses. The unions were not forgotten and were the subject of a special presentation on which certain of them reported to their principals in terms which expressed, at the very least, a wait-and-see neutrality.[3]

THE SHARING OF KNOWLEDGE

In order to sanction the massive support given to the main results of the business review, it was decided to send out a questionnaire to 40,000 of the company's employees. This short questionnaire, containing 19 questions two of which were 'open', allowed everybody to express themselves on the principal observations and, at the end, freely to put forward suggestions for improvement. Once again, there was great surprise. There where the prophets of doom and gloom were predicting a poor return, disinterest from personnel, close to 20,000 replies were received, thereby posing the technical problem of how to process them. The open questions were scrutinised, in the boardroom, by volunteer employees from different parts of the organisation and working without time limits on the questionnaires. The main results were communicated to the rest of the employees through the intermediary of a 'journal on the debate' created for this purpose by the new director of human resources, in charge of the operation. They showed, in addition to a massive support of observations, a surprising availability for investing themselves concretely in the search for solutions and, if these appeared justified to them, a great openness faced with the possible sacrifices that might be asked of them. Nothing naïve in all that. It was in fact a quid pro quo situation – the employees did not intend to limit their involvement to replying to surveys or questionnaires which would justify decisions which they would have no option other than to accept. They clearly wanted to go further and to be able to propose their own ideas on a new organisation of work, on new practices, or even changes to structures. It was this package which was proposed in a referendum, fortunately an exceptional procedure in a company and which had the positive results that we all know. This consultation, carried out in a context of transparency, helped to build an agreement between the employees and their executives, focusing at the same time on the *process of change and its methodology*, and on what, in exchange for this different way of working with them, the employees were prepared to accept. This was not in any way a blank cheque made out the management team, as shown by subsequent events.

THE SEARCH FOR SOLUTIONS

It was on the basis of this agreement that an impressive number of task forces were set up in the company to take charge of the 'processes' that appeared to be posing the most problems. Their functioning was particularly innovative. Each process was reviewed from the *customer's point of view*, as revealed by a specialised agency. The idea was simple, even though it still remained barely understood: if one wants actors to work on new methods of functioning, there must be something which gives meaning to such a change, failing which the debate becomes theoretical, abstract and ideological. In an organisation such as this one, as well as in most others, it is the customer who provides meaning: first of all because it is the customer who gives the company a living, but mostly because, as soon as one 'pulls the thread', one discovers *an ocean of possible different practices* that nobody could even have imagined. To sum up, starting from the customer is starting from the end result since, for the customer, this is the only thing that counts, while segmented areas are only interested in specific results.[4]

In parallel, these task forces were 'nurtured'. To start with, they were not built in line with any 'political' logic, in other words, including actors purely because it was tactically important for them to be there, but instead their work was fed from the detailed results of business reviews carried out previously. This meant that discussions were continually refocused on the existing reality and on the means of creating a different one. In this phase, the inventiveness of those involved showed itself to be extreme, in the same way that the emergence was seen of personalities, who had previously been condemned to stay out of sight by the company's traditional methods of functioning. Categories which until then had ignored or scorned each other now started to talk, not for any reason of comradeship, but because the necessity was apparent, in the name of this new logic anchored on the customer, of bringing together what had until then been kept apart in the name of a logic of formality or technicality. It was these task forces that provided the bulk of the proposals and recommendations that were subsequently implemented.

Forming and coordinating the task forces was, as a general rule, a key factor in the success of this type of procedure. In the very 'political' tradition of French companies, the development of such groups was the subject of very particular attention so as to avoid upsetting anybody with the way in which they were made up. But, quite naturally, since such groups are formed on a political basis, they do what they were designed to do – politics. This way of doing things must and can be reappraised based on the introduction of the customer logic which brings to light the new collaborations that are necessary. Similarly, the coordination of such groups must leave nothing to chance. What is meant here by 'nurture' is the fact of not allowing their work to be boiled down to an exchange of impressions or diffused feelings. It must be oriented and steered around shared observations, established facts not mere anecdotes. Such methods have always aroused the enthusiasm of those involved, no doubt because of their capacity to take the drama out of debates and thus encourage further work on them.

In the case of Air France, it would be naïve to think that everything took place without incident and in a atmosphere of frankness and openness. Nothing removes the effects of taking sides in an organisation. Power struggles remain the same and the defence of sectional interests does not just fade away overnight by some miracle. In the same way, not all suggestions were put into application, in fact far from it. But it is the new process itself, far more open and trusting, more risky as well, that made it possible to take decisions which, until then, had been rejected without even looking at them.

WHAT LESSONS CAN BE DRAWN FROM THE 'AIR FRANCE' CASE?

We therefore need to stand back a little and look at the main characteristics of this approach to change, and see whether they can be generalised in terms of steering an action of this type. There are four major points for discussion: The first involves steering by *method* and not by substance or procedures. And it is certainly not by chance that one speaks of 'method X' to designate what was done in this company. Here, the word must be understood in its true meaning of a way of proceeding, as opposed to a precise and serene knowledge of what must be done to the basis of things. Everybody in the company had an evident awareness that fundamental changes were necessary. This did not necessarily mean that they were possible or even that the *moment of change had arrived*. To reach this stage, it was necessary to change the deal, not just by immediately proposing solutions that nobody would have believed in, nor by drawing up a complete action plan covering all the aspects identified as needing modification. Such an approach would certainly have been doomed to failure through its lack of credibility and firm foundation in reality. What was done here was to think things through differently, starting from a procedure which did not really take into account the sector's specificities – which everybody had always tended to exaggerate – but which proposed *steps*. These focused less on the progress of change itself than on the progressive involvement of all actors in the process. Regaining the trust of employees first of all required that they should be shown trust, which was in fact what happened.

The first of these steps was an *investment in knowledge* which, as we will see, does not need to be exhaustive, provided it makes it possible to highlight the key points of the actors' reality, and to understand the problems behind the symptoms. We have seen that the previous situation was, to the contrary, a situation of *ignorance*. This is an endemic disease in companies which often do not see the necessity of knowledge and prefer to devote the best part of their resources and energy to solutions. They invest in collecting data which is attractive by its abundance, they gather 'information', 'advice' and 'opinions', they rarely build a true knowledge base. It should be said that their usual consultants hardly encourage them in this, especially since building up such a knowledge base does not give them much in return, and also they only rarely have the necessary training. Notwithstanding the fact that the solutions so quickly found in this manner are not generally suitable and try to resolve problems that nobody knows about, they produce unpleasant side effects. They come into conflict with actors who do not know what one is trying to remedy; they make them feel guilty by expecting them to change their practices even when they have the impression they are already doing their best; they aggravate conflictual situations and phenomena of resistance. In brief, the cure is worse than the ill.

The knowledge built up in this way has been *shared*. Such sharing is one of the exercises that arouses the most reluctance from executives. In fact, they cannot imagine that their employees might be ready to accept the reality that a serious survey shows to them. They suspect them of obscurantism and escapism when faced with the facts. This is total nonsense. On the one hand, because experience shows that, as soon as actors have the feeling that what they are being told is not partisan, that not only is it taken from what they themselves have said but also that thorough work has made it possible *to add value* to their own arguments, they discover that they have been listened to, in the deepest sense of the term. They are thus enabled to understand their own vague feelings on things, to tie this in to a vaster whole which gives them a sense of direction and shows that they are not being made to bear an individual responsibility which is not their own. On the other hand, because trying to flee from reality is more the state of the managers themselves, often frightened by realising that what they are supposed to be managing is in fact to a great extent escaping from their control and, in any case, does not function at all in the manner claimed by official rhetoric. It is surprising to see, once a survey of this type is proposed, to what extent appeals for caution are multiplied, to what point even the most authoritarian bosses can do little to get their reluctant senior executives to accept this investigation. And yet none of them has any hesitation in communicating and circulating their organisation charts! This means that people are quite willing to discuss theory, but rarely practice. Contrary to a preconceived idea, the company is an empire of abstraction as soon as its real method of functioning is involved.[5] But what everybody accommodates themselves to in normal times can become a severe handicap when it is necessary to change things, for this fear when faced with what is real is *infantilising* for actors who reject it.

In addition, sharing knowledge is the start of trust, while most organisations are places of distrust. In the same way that one finds it difficult to accept that everything is not planned in advance, because one fears what the actors are going to do with the margins of freedom allowed to them, one also remains perplexed as to the way in which they will use the knowledge that is given to them. 'Empowerment' – since that is what this is – is a fascinating subject for seminars, an inexhaustible theme for articles, and a far more painful procedure.

What does this mean, in fact? That one has given the actors the necessary resources and elements for getting away from their partial vision of reality, in order to understand their side of things thanks to a grasp of the whole picture, that one enables them to go beyond the anecdotes and reach the facts. This is the way in which they acquire *more power*, which is indeed the literal translation of the word. And this power, they are going to use it, which rouses all sorts of fears, such as intelligence generally arouses. For orienting this use of their power in a positive direction for the organisation is not easy, to the extent that, the more armed the actors are, the less likely they are to accept without argument doing what they are told to do, with the partisan and ideological speeches which usually seem to accompany injunctions. It is essential to reckon *with them* and not without them or against them.

It is for this reason that the last part of the strategy of implementation, as we have been able to observe at Air France, consisted of associating the highest possible number of actors with the search for solutions. One can see an interesting paradox. It often happens that executives, who in fact do nothing to hide this, call in top consultancy firms, of world renown, to 'legitimise' their decisions. A 'recommendation' proposed by X, top expert on the subject, cannot be argued with. And yet it is, without hesitation, as soon as the actors find it unjustified because it generally makes them bear the total cost of change. However, what better and more fundamental legitimisation can exist than that provided by the interested parties themselves, when they are asked to find solutions to problems that they understand and share? Certainly they will find more practical and concrete solutions than any outside consultant, provided they are given a little help. In any case, they will *open the way to* such solutions. On this subject Schein states: 'If you give people knowledge of the way that they are linked to one another and in which their whole system functions, they have the capability of perceiving what must be changed, and they do not need you to suggest to them a model of what is not right and the way in which you are going to change it.'[6] It is this model of trust which is best able to unblock the most strained situations and to make acceptable what one would never have dared imagine.

GENERAL TRUST AND INDIVIDUAL TRUST

Yet it is necessary to see that the strategy of change proposed here is far from being universally accepted, and that it is no doubt closely linked to the European context in which it has been developed and in which most of the examples given have taken place. It favours participation, the human factor, the search for support from the greatest number. In fact, it involves trust at two levels. The first is general and postulates that one can trust the actors to understand situations provided they are given access to knowledge; starting from that point, they will accept these situations and will help in searching for solutions which are not solely partisan, even if these solutions can sometimes, briefly, be unfavourable to them. One thus creates the conditions for an implicit exchange in which the actors can give their agreement to measures that, at other times, they would have rejected, because, first, one has decided to tell them the why and wherefore of things and has relied on them to find the way out and, second, they expect an improvement in the future, which will include salvaging their own situation.

But there is also individual trust, from day to day, the trust involved in the hierarchical relationship, which, when effective, helps to avoid many dramas and makes change possible on a day-to-day basis. Jean-François Manzoni and Jean-Louis Barsoux have tried to define the five conditions for trust in discussions between managers and subordinates. What they point out is not surprising: in their opinion, the boss must first of all create an atmosphere that is favourable to discussion; both sides must reach agreement on the problem's symptoms; they should next arrive at a mutual understanding of what is causing poor performance in certain areas; they should then agree on performance objectives and their intention to continue the relationship; finally they should consent to communicate more openly in the future.[7] From this point of view, trust is more formalised, more 'contractualised' than we have developed here. But the idea is the same and favours the game of 'openness' as opposed to distrust, indifference or suddenness.

THE CORRELATION OF STRATEGIES FOR CHANGE

However, it is necessary to see that the strategy of change proposed here is being universally accepted, but, by standing back slightly from the situation, one can see that the requirements of the modern world, such as the sudden acceleration of economic cycles, which is seen in the appearance and rapid disappearance of many companies and in the growing importance accorded to satisfying the shareholder, are leading to the opposition of two theories and therefore two practices of change.[8]

The first is diametrically opposed to what has just been put forward in this chapter. Specialists call it the E theory, because it gives absolute priority in action to the economic value. They are in agreement in recognising that it is 'hard' since it considers that the only legitimate measurement of the company's success is the value created for the shareholder. In a process of change, this involves the massive use of financial incentives, resorting drastically and without scruple to lay-offs, to downsizing, to restructuring – all of which so marked the end of the twentieth century. This is of course characteristic of the North American world and insistently sends us back to the practices that a certain number of writers have no hesitation in considering as the key factor for the United States' success compared with the rest of the developed world.

The O theory, given this name because it favours organisational capability, is far more widespread in Asia and in Europe. Nobody will be surprised to see that this is close to what was done in the Air France example. The goal that is generally pursued is to develop what is usually called a 'company culture' by investing in human capabilities through an individual and organisational learning process. In most cases, companies adopt this when, prior to the appearance of the need to change, there existed an implicit contract of loyalty–protection between them and their employees – this was indeed the case for Air France – and where the abrupt termination of this contract would carry serious risks of the organisation finally exploding. Underlying this situation, one can see that what is favoured in this approach is maintaining strong links over time between the company and the people working in it. One might even think that the more such links are woven over a long period of time, by little successive touches, by obtaining ever more advantages, the more resorting to 'soft' strategy becomes necessary, even if this causes further deteriorate in the situation.[9]

Indeed, these two approaches are even more different than they appear at first look on six key points:

- The goals which, as we have seen, are, in the first theory, to maximise return on short-term investment for the shareholder and, in the second theory, to develop organisational capabilities. Here, we find a classic distinction on something that we have already highlighted[10] and which, if we put the customer alongside the shareholder, allows us to set the logic of the assignment (E theory) against the logic of the organisation (O theory). One can understand why the more bureaucratic things become – priority given to their own constraints – that is, the more importance is given to protections available to their members, the more they will push towards the second option.

- Leading change which, in the E theory, will be carried out by commands from the top, and which members of the organisation will obey without questioning their validity or their consequences. This can be seen every day in the North American world without provoking any more reaction than that. To the contrary, as we have seen above, the O theory will encourage everybody's involvement, in line with the modalities that we have attempted to point out.

- In the E theory, priority will be given to what one calls 'systems' in the Anglo-Saxon sense of structures, rules and procedures, based on the belief, solidly anchored on strict methods of control, that the actors are indeed doing what such systems enjoin them to do. Curiously, this returns us to the initial dream of a bureaucracy – this time in the conventional sense of the term – as thought of by Max Weber and which would be an organisation capable of producing general and impersonal rules as well as applying them: this is only possible with the backing of a severe system of sanctions. The O approach, seen from this point of view, is more pragmatic and corresponds partly to what has been discussed in the first part of this book: what one proposes to change as a priority are the *behaviours* of actors rather than their attitudes, by creating new contexts for them. Here, the systems are used as levers, in a perspective which is itself *systemic*, but in the sociological sense of the term. One wagers on the playing capabilities of these actors, rather than on their diligence to follow, to the letter, what is laid down in writing.

- The process will be different. In comparison with what was observed in the transport company – which is nevertheless European – this will consist, in the E theory, of drawing up plans and programmes that are as accurate, comprehensive and restrictive as possible, but, this time, making sure of their effective and rapid implementation. The O vision will favour experimentation, evaluation, comings and goings between the goals to be achieved and the results observed, and then generalisation even if this means continually watching that the necessary adaptations are made.

- The levers used will not be the same, nor will they be used in the same way. The E strategy will focus on monetary incentives, linking them directly to short-term financial results, such that stock market rates will allow them to be continually evaluated and considered to be incontestable. We have virtually come back to a 'Taylorist' vision of the motivation of individuals at work. In the O strategy, the financial rewards are used more to accompany change than to produce it. But, above all, it is the overall tools in a human resource management policy – appraisals, promotions, assignments, pay packages – which will be used here as levers for change Of course, the more the organisation tends to rigidify these in an earlier phase, the more their implementation will be delicate and will require negotiation with the interested parties.

- In both cases, calling in outside consultants takes on different meanings. In the first case (E theory), it is they who analyse the problems – in fact, focus most of the time on the symptoms – who sketch out solutions and look after the implementation of their own recommendations. All the big consultancy firms have drawn up methodologies on this point which can easily be duplicated. In the second case (O theory), the consultants are a support mechanism, appear as facilitators who help not only management – as Beer and Nohria seem to want – but also, as we have tried to show, all personnel to find their own solutions, which will then be the subject of a formal validation by those in charge. But the – slight – distinction that we have just introduced with regard to those who need to be really supported and helped, closes the loop: it shows that trust, as accorded to all those who are involved in a process of change, is still far from being universally admitted.

7 The Particular Case of Public Organisations

Public organisations present an interesting paradox from the point of view of change.[1] On the one hand, their reform is on the agenda in the principal industrialised countries, for reasons that are easy to understand – they will not be able to escape from the fundamental changes that one is seeing across the world and which concern all organisations, whether public or private; however, on the other hand, nowhere has this reform been carried out very convincingly or, if so, then in the greatest difficulty.

Such changes, which we have already had the opportunity to describe,[2] occur under the impact of globalisation which, on a daily basis, is showing itself in a growing pressure from the customer or from the user to bring costs down and improve the quality of goods produced or services sold. The result is a veritable revolution in organisations which does not express itself solely in the notorious reorganisations so loudly applauded by the world's main stock markets. This involves radical changes in the job sector within all developed countries. On one side, the concrete methods of working are very rapidly redefined with regard to hourly, weekly or annual rhythms as well as to relational modes with others; on another side, the link to the organisation and to the company in particular is 'jeopardised' in some way, and not only with regard to the situation on the job market, completely shelving the celebrated loyalty–protection exchange that has characterised the salary relationship from the beginning of the century until the middle of the 1980s.[3]

In parallel, the highly differentiated intensity of the desire to change displayed by the different countries expresses the difficulty of this task. This ranges from high and sometimes single-minded commitment, as is the case in the United Kingdom, through to a situation in which the word caution is a euphemism (France, for example), not forgetting countries which, in the image of Sweden or Germany, have made the choice in their strategy of privileging experimentation, tests, and then their generalisation. Similarly, one sees the appearance of substantial differences between those which put the accent on the managerial dimension of change, thus emphasising the sometimes astonishing deficiencies in the matter of public bodies, and those which focus on the processes and try to rebuild them into a new logic, at the risk of reproducing the mistake of confusing the rule and its clarity with the real functioning that is obtained.

But, whatever the strategic choices made, none of the countries involved has had an easy task of it, once this has meant implementing real change, even if most of the actors concerned contest neither the urgency of reforms nor the need to change profoundly public organisations' methods of functioning. Here, we see a case in which there is a distancing between what the actors can understand and what they can accept, between what a good strategy makes it possible to predict, negotiate and announce, and the possibility of implementation. Everywhere, we find difficulty, conflicts, then negotiations which do not stem from an abstract resistance to changes, but rather to the issues of such changes. If these issues are not properly understood, pushing such organisations towards a very specific problematic and strategy, far from any technocratic or ideological approach, the transformation of public administrations runs the risk of finally showing itself to be more costly than expected in human and financial terms, especially, of course, in countries where it is the subject of the strongest misgivings.

THE STUMBLING BLOCK OF LEGAL AND LEGALISTIC VISIONS

A first difficulty is quick to appear: the very strong legalistic or legal cultures, which characterise most of our countries, have dramatically boosted the confusion between organisation and structure, where we have seen to what extent this handicaps the actual problematic of change. This is easy to understand in the administrative world, marked simultaneously by legalism, Weberian tradition in terms of how the State is designed and the chronic absence of management culture. The consequence of this has been the usual assimilation of reform with change of structures, and the transformation of policies of change into a more or less skilful and well-founded reconstruction of the administrative Meccano. But the effect was worse here than elsewhere, for these areas are where territorial defence is at its fiercest. This concerns not only senior executives but also union organisations, as we have shown in the previous chapter with the example of the French tax authorities. Doing this reinforces the factors of blockage, sometimes irreversibly, and the actors only become more reluctant to launch themselves into an adventure which they believe lost in advance, educated as they are by the trials and tribulations of their predecessors.

NEITHER STRUCTURES, NOR RULES

One can only be surprised by the blindness of so many public reformers, and their inability to observe that the interest focused on structures was on the decline in other areas, to the profit of that focused on real methods of functioning, such as already defined. This understanding of organisations on a simple mode, as if formed from the way that people work, make decisions, solve their problems, cooperate or not, in brief, like a set of rational strategies from intelligent actors, makes it easier to understand and therefore anticipate the difficulties encountered. They stem from the particular characteristics of public authorities as distinct from organisations, and therefore from the levers on which one can act to make them change, which are more limited and more difficult to manipulate *because, precisely, over time, the members of these organisations and their representatives have fought to protect themselves against their possible use*. There is, therefore, a need to lay out what characterises such areas and makes change both so necessary and so perilous.

What defines the functioning of public authorities is neither fundamentally nor principally the corpus of rules which govern them, but the application which has been made of them over time and which, in many countries, has resulted in a multitude of local, specific, particular agreements. These have always had as an objective the increase of the protection, of any kind, from which the members of such organisations benefit, whether this involves protections faced with customers or users on whom one has imposed one's rhythm and one's constraints, faced with bosses whose real power has been reduced to nothing by the impressive array of rules and procedures, which have gradually taken the place of the hierarchy, or even faced with others, with one's peers and one's colleagues, thanks to the segmentation around the succession of tasks which has allowed everybody to protect themselves from the demands and constraints of cooperation. From this point of view, one can say that public organisations are in essence bureaucratic and that this comprises the major difficulty in their real and fundamental change.

WHAT IS A BUREAUCRACY?

Bureaucratic is not used here in the polemic sense of an organisation that would always produce more paper and would be slow, heavy and not very responsive. This word is meant to emphasise a far more fundamental phenomenon which is at the very heart of difficulties in change for administrative bodies: *A bureaucracy is an organisation that is characterised by the fact that all the criteria that it uses are endogenous*. To say this in more simple terms, it is an entity which, in all its acts, gives priority to its own problems, whether technical or human, as opposed to those in its environment.

This form of organisation corresponded to a certain time in contemporary history, which was characterised by the general scarcity of goods and services that the citizens of developed countries aspired to consume: either material goods to which industrial mass production corresponded, or services among which those provided by agencies under State control were not the least important, in order to ensure both social order and State of law. Max Weber in his time, together with Jeremy Rifkin or Robert Reich today, have very clearly described the issues and modalities of this period:[4] For Max Weber, as for Henri Mintzberg, the word 'bureaucratic' conjures up a collective order, a legitimate domination founded on a set of rules and procedures, a professional and process organisation.

Such a mode of action must also be applied in the same way to those governed by the bureaucracy as to its own members. Virtuous towards its 'subjects' because it establishes and ensures the equality of all under law, bureaucracy is also virtuous towards its members whom again it manages on a principle of strict equality – at least in appearance – which little by little excludes differentiation, judgement, evaluation on the basis of results obtained compared with the expectations of those being served, all of these being things which, in modern administrative language, can be summed up by the word 'arbitrary'. The strongly pejorative connotation of this word in these areas, while in fact it only expresses recourse to free will, shows clearly to what extent human intervention – judgemental, prejudiced – is rejected to the profit of uniformity and conformity.

THE PROTECTION FUNCTION

In fact, looking closely, such principles of action, of which nobody contests the initial legitimacy, have led to a maximisation in these organisations of the function of work protection which has been mentioned in earlier chapters. To the three traditional protections – against life, against customers, against peers – has now been added that against hierarchy, against the boss who makes judgements, who grades or appraises. One can understand without much difficulty why changing such organisations poses even more problems than for any others, to the extent that their endogenous natures are developed to the extreme, and that union organisations have given themselves the task of defending them at any price, often excluding any other consideration of cost, effectiveness or adaptation to world changes.

Nonetheless, over time, doubts arose on the virtues and effectiveness of such methods of functioning. Quite naturally, such doubts came to light at the end of the 1970s, when the resources available to States for feeding the onward progress of such organisations and for amassing the resources that they distributed to society – which conferred upon them their legitimacy and led tax-paying citizens to close their eyes – dried up. If one adds to this the 'capillarity effect', that is, the rapid transformation of organisations acting on the market, and therefore the possibility for the citizen-customer to compare the way in which he is treated by the various organisations, we see the striking appearance of two features of public bureaucracies: they distribute services that are of universally poor quality but at a very high cost. However, this dual observation of the 'extra cost of poor service' is closely linked to the endogenous features of the administrative services mentioned above. To understand this, let us try to highlight the two constraints to which administrative bodies traditionally give priority when designing their methods of functioning.

WHAT MAKES UP THE EXTRA COST OF POOR SERVICE?

The first is strict compliance with the succession and specialisation of tasks. In a still widely predominant Taylorist logic, production of the service is broken down into 'successive acts' and the organisation reproduces, even in its structures, this sequential logic. One can easily anticipate the advantages and disadvantages of this method of functioning. Advantages for members of the organisation: *they do not have to cooperate*. They simply pass around *files* once they have, at their speed, dealt with their share of them, thus avoiding any situation of dependency in relation to one another. Again, it is this protection function in relation to peers, colleagues, others in general which it is absolutely essential to understand. This has been built up over time, based on a slow adaptation of the initial rules of personnel management. This has tended continually to reduce the involvement of others in one's own work, as it has, little by little, nullified the powers of the hierarchy in terms of remuneration, grading, appraisal or career development for agents, yet again reinforcing their real autonomy. We can never repeat enough that, at least in the French case – but this is less isolated than one might think – it is not the general status of the public function which renders adaptation of administrations particularly arduous, but the use which has been made of it since the end of World War II. It is this internal constraint which has always been the second most important priority for administrative bodies.

So, advantages for the agents, but disadvantages (and sometimes major ones) for tax- and rate-paying citizens and the community as a whole. First, because this method of functioning badly affects the quality of the service: it produces slowness, waste, error and above all irresponsibility, to the extent that nobody is accountable for the end result to the customer. The latter must try to find his way through a jungle of tasks and segmentation, face up to the 'monsters' which sometimes emerge after the thoughtless stringing together of actions that have been blindly carried out. In brief, he must follow the 'bureaucratic path' of an organisation which has shaped itself around its own needs instead of the needs of those whom it is supposed to serve. The example of the reimbursement of VAT credit, given in Chapter 2, is just one illustration. But we must repeat that all this is linked to the *bureaucratic form of the work and not the public nature of the organisation*. This has only been involved through the policy of the employer-State, which has only rarely measured the impact, on the service and on its cost, of the successive advantages conceded to its employees, and even more so because long periods of political instability have not favoured an integrated vision of public action.[5] However, examples seen towards the end of the 1990s, particularly in the United Kingdom, have shown that the privatisation of a State service is not in itself the guarantee of greater efficiency: changing the methods of functioning is not enough.

Alongside the poor quality of services offered by this type of organisation, we also find the extra cost that it generates. Protection from others – the fierce desire not to be dependent upon them – always involves the consumption of additional resources: being autonomous presupposes the means for such autonomy and hence the multiplication of equipment and agents, offices, computers, photocopiers – in brief, everything that contributes to life in an autarchy, assimilated here to life free of all conditions. One might find it difficult to understand why, in the trading world in general and the car industry in particular, it is through a ceaseless concentration on transforming organisations – in the meaning given to this expression since the beginning of this book – and concretely by introducing always more in the way of cooperation, that production costs have been drastically reduced, but without the public organisations having to follow the same process in order to produce the same improvements. Or, in other words, using an analogy which is dear to us, it is highly probable that the reduction in hospital spending, in countries such as France or Belgium, would doubtless be far more effective if it were based on a fundamental transformation of the working methods of hospital doctors among themselves and therefore on a reconstruction of the hospital around the patient, instead of on a strictly financial and bureaucratic control of medical treatment.

DOING MORE WITH LESS

What has been said here has never been properly understood by the civil servants themselves as well as by the political governing bodies. In a high proportion of countries, the equation of public services remains the same: if one wants better quality of service, one must devote more resources to it – and always more resources for always more quality. It is of little consequence that pupil numbers are dropping – increasing the number of teachers is still a guarantee of quality for those who remain.

This logic has no end to it and it maintains a vicious circle that can paradoxically be observed in the most liberal as well as the most conservative countries in terms of State reform: as strong pressure is exerted in order to reduce public spending, cuts are made mechanically and often without discernment in the workforces. Such cuts are made without affecting the methods of functioning; that is, without using the levers that might lead actors to develop other strategies than those aimed to protect themselves or, to put it plainly, to cooperate more. The result is a deterioration in the services provided which increases not only the public's discontent but also and above all the frustration of agents who, taken individually, feel they are doing the best they can with the poor resources available to them. For it is true that, in administrations which do not understand the organisational dimension of quality and cost reduction, one is always obliged to call for greater goodwill and individual dedication – veritable safety valves for the system's inefficiency.

From this point, it is only by relying on public irritation that agents will obtain, as a matter of urgency and precipitation, the additional resources that will enable them to continue working in a segmented and uncooperative environment. Such unwillingness to understand is a paralysing situation in a country like France. In others, to the contrary – Australia, for example – it has led to a drastic reduction in the size of administrative entities, reconstructed around the customer–service rendered relationship, as well as to the introduction of a true logic for personnel management, which has given true margins for manoeuvre to supervisors. One can also see that countries which are not in a position to offer the same margins for manoeuvre to their supervisory staff are starting to suffer from a veritable 'vocation crisis', which is resulting in serious difficulties, not only for recruiting but also winning the loyalty of their managers, especially senior executives.

What seems to be at issue is no longer the difference in remuneration between the public and private sectors, but rather the absence of prospects, which characterises the public sector and which is apparent on a day-to-day basis in the impossibility of introducing any reform whatsoever, while the trading sector shows evidence of extreme vitality. One encounters, here, the paradox of over-protection that characterises such organisations: by trying to do too much in this context, they end up by only attracting or keeping people who have the greatest need for such protections; that is, to be quite blunt, neither the best nor the most dynamic.[6]

A GENERAL REAPPRAISAL

At this turn of the century, it is therefore this extra cost of poor service which makes the reform of public organisations so essential, and indeed inevitable, just about everywhere in the world. The competition in allocating State resources is becoming increasingly keen, at the same time that new tax policies for reducing compulsory payments are making these same resources scarcer. Finally, the idea that only the public sector will be able to escape the general reappraisal of organisations, which has been a feature of recent years, is more and more untenable, even if, on this subject, people's feelings are sometimes ambiguous.[7] All this leads progressively to the idea that what has been possible in the trading sector, *doing more and better with less*, should also be possible in the public sector.

We can add to this what we have earlier called the capillarity effect, which means that the user/customer cannot continue to accept the ever-growing qualitative distance between the product and service offered to him by an increasing proportion of suppliers, and what he obtains from everything to do with the public domain: individualisation of service, immediateness of response, fair pricing and so on are today at the heart of taxpayer/customer expectations. If the gap between what is supplied by both domains was to grow any wider, it is the political market which would then sanction the administrative world, even if, for the time being, in countries such as France, it has demonstrated the greatest reluctance to do so.

DIFFICULTY IN CHANGING PUBLIC ORGANISATIONS

The forced privatisation of whole sections of public services in the Anglo-Saxon countries falls within this type of sanction. But, with a little hindsight, one might consider that this involves attempts similar, although more brutal and radical, to those that the de Gaullian reformism of the 1960s had tried to impose on France through the creation of semi-public agencies, for dealing with the most crucial problems in the country's modernisation.

The creation of the Agence Nationale pour l'Emploi[8] obeyed this logic. Its relative lack of success, at least in terms of imposing a new type of administrative action, shows that institutional intention is not, in itself, enough to produce change.

Indeed, if one lines up what have been identified as the dominant features of public bureaucracies and the new pressures that are exerted on them, one sees the first signs that these are the basic difficulties facing any true attempts at change in administrative areas. These are first *intellectual* and, for the most part, stem from the training received by public sector employees, dominated overwhelmingly by a narrow legalism which is truly the administrative version of Taylor's scientific organisation of industrial work: the organisation around a succession of tasks, as initially expounded by Taylor, is perceived by its practitioners as being of a virtually scientific nature, and hence the only one possible. The question which the reformer asks himself therefore becomes 'Is it possible to do things differently?' However, this 'differently' entails acceptance of the modes of action which are, for the most part, very distant from the culture and dominant practices of these bodies and from legalistic rhetoric. It is necessary to introduce some fuzziness into the definition of tasks, which is only possible if it is accompanied by methods of appraisal, individually or collectively, that prevent it from being a factor of increased irresponsibility; in the same way, redundancy and conflicts – in the sociological sense of the term – make their appearance, a situation which is poorly tolerated in organisations where the general interest should be to federate, at the same time as reducing any divergence. From this point of view, this is indeed a transition from *legalism to management*, and certain countries have fully understood this, making it the predominant orientation of their strategies for reform.[9]

But the difficulties confronting change are just as practical and often more prosaic. *It is a matter of reversing the predominant habit of doing things, not necessarily better but always with more.* The link between quality and abundance of resources is at the heart of the problematic of public services. We will mention here the *abundance of resources consumed*, a situation not necessarily perceived by those who consume them, with segmentation and compartmentalisation making everybody blind and producing virtually invisible effects of wastage: when the parents, teachers and pupils of a high school in the south of France were clamouring for an additional supervisor for their school, and were forced to occupy the premises in order to bring their problem to the attention of the authorities, no doubt they were aware of a cruel lack of resources; but at the same time, when one looks at the National Education budget and the proportion of people in this administration who actually stand in front of the pupils, one cannot help a feeling of wastefulness and the impression of an organisation which is going to the dogs in terms of managing its human resources.

PROTECTION FUNCTION AND PRODUCTION FUNCTION

Despite these examples which help one to understand that there is no contradiction between individual irritation and the formidable collective wastage, one can indeed speak of a *comfort relationship* with regard to these organisations. which makes it possible to promise more, on condition that the cost of this more is externalised onto the institution and not borne by the members of the organisation itself, through new methods of work. If it is really necessary to do more with less, which is the predominant contemporary trend, it is a radical change – and therefore no doubt costly in human terms – of the methods of functioning that is required. One can understand from this that the reluctance of agents and their management is not a matter of abstract and theoretical resistance to change. It is one of the manifestations, more accentuated in the public sector for the reasons which have just been stated, of the transformation of work functions in our developed societies. The famous *protection function* is being gradually and *painfully* wiped out to the profit of the *production function. This mission logic*, forcing one to turn one's routing operating methods towards the customer, towards the customer's expectations in terms of quality and cost, wins over the endogenous logic of the organisation and its members. Under pressure from all the factors mentioned above, *precariousness* is gaining ground everywhere, including in the public sector. In the case of administration employees, this does not mean a precariousness on the job market, but rather a redefinition of the conditions of employment within these organisations; conditions which were until then very advantageous since far more oriented towards the agents themselves than towards those at whom the services produced were aimed. We must see *simultaneity, cooperation, divergence of interest under the spotlight*, which cannot take place without some ups and downs. It is easy to understand that, if one is not in a position to offer an alternative, a 'new deal' to those whose agreement linking them to their employer-State has just been brutally destroyed, it will be even more difficult to get them to accept the necessary reforms.

WHAT STRATEGY FOR CHANGE?

This raises the problem of the *strategy for change*, which here seems rather the same as that already mentioned for the transport company.[10]

Until then, the dialogue – when it exists – has been reduced to only the representative organisations, real institutional relays for personnel management. However, the great majority of these are not and cannot be in favour of such reforms, to the extent that they are structured and organised in line with the conventional segmentations and working methods that are associated with them. Any reappraisal of any of these is a potential danger, including for implicit share-outs of territories, which are carried out over time between such organisations.[11]

The general main themes – sometimes abstract in their concrete consequences on daily life – which until then united public sector employees, whatever their job category, like the public service or the general interest, are today paradoxically becoming more concrete, because the public is asking for accounts on their real meaning and their implications for the public. Because of this, not everything is defendable at the same time or for all. In the interest of citizens, it is more and more difficult not to match the opening hours of administrative offices with the times when people can go there; it is less and less legitimate to maintain a centralised personnel management, when needs are becoming more and more qualitative and diversified. In brief, the traditional modalities of action for the most conservative union organisations have been hit head-on and made more rigid, even though experience shows that the agents themselves are far more aware of the transformations needed and certainly far more prepared to accept them – under certain conditions of course.

STARTING FROM THE AGENTS THEMSELVES

This sends us back to the question of *trust* tackled in Chapter 6. It is still less in the traditions of the administrative world than in those of the trading sector. From a certain point of view, for the senior executives of public organisations, the professional reality of the agents does not exist. There are rules and procedures, which people are all the more willing to believe are applied since they are supposed to guarantee equality for all under the law. Apart from that, there are only the union organisations, reduced to a social dialogue – which is becoming increasingly impoverished, occasionally puerile, and in any case dissociated from reality and without tangible results. Paradoxically, most actors are more or less in agreement on this observation but do not see the means for getting out of the situation, which more and more resembles a zero-sum game, in which change becomes less and less playable for unions that are more and more strained over previous situations and where agents have an ingrained feeling that they are not being listened to.

act, above and beyond the management awareness to which the training programme can lay claim.

Such levers, which must aim to put the actors of public administrations into new contexts and thus change their behaviours – their strategies – are mainly a matter for human resource management systems. However, the very development of such systems over time has tended to neutralise their impact on the differentiation of individuals and therefore deprive them of the managerial role that was originally attributed to them. This leads to three observations.

We have already noted that, to date, one has never seen a change in a bureaucracy's method of functioning, whether in the public or the private sector, without a fundamental change to its human resource management systems, by introducing randomness, differentiation, room for the manager's appraisal, even subjective, of people of whom he is in charge, and based on whose action he is himself assessed. The modification of such systems and the sometimes fierce opposition that this arouses are indeed part of the movement to dilute the employment protection function that was analysed above. Progress in this area can only be slow and negotiated with the agents themselves.

The privatisation or sub-contracting of public services is a way of getting round the obstacle which, as we have already seen, is not new. The acknowledgement that we find behind this strategy is in fact that the difference between the private and public sectors is based principally on the level of protection offered to employees, and hence on the degree of constraints that can be imposed on them, particularly in terms of working conditions. The wager which is made here is that change in public organisations is an illusion or at least that it requires so much time and effort that it does not fall within the deadlines that necessity demands. It is therefore necessary to go through the process of their disappearance and replacement. The consequence of this is sometimes to leave, in what is left of the traditional administrations, only the most insignificant tasks with low added value. Defenders of the public service should reflect on this apparent paradox: the intransigent conservatism sometimes demonstrated by them has a chance of reducing this sector to what is least interesting, least valued, least lucrative.

This is why some countries, in France's case some ministries, have chosen to negotiate, step by step, towards a development, even moderate, not of statutes, but of their application, making it possible to reintroduce the idea and practice of management and responsibility in the management of agents. It is remarkable to see that, in a country so little open to the idea of administrative reform as France, it is in the Ministry of Public Works that the most significant progress has been accomplished. However, this Ministry is, at the same time, the one with the highest proportion of its activity taking place on the competitive market. Here again, necessity makes the rules.

The final key point which must be tackled in terms of change in administrative organisations is change in structures. This has not been dealt with until now because the thesis of this book is precisely that change in organisation is not principally change in structures. But countries such as Australia or New Zealand have shown that there are alternative structures to those based on the strict succession of tasks, the adoption of which is a determining complement to the efforts which are made in terms of renewal and modernisation of agent management. The operations and delivery services show that even an administrative world can be designed around a user logic and the translation of such a logic into routine methods of functioning. However, this involves abandoning the idea of integrated and undifferentiated 'administrative mega organisations'.

In fact, progress is made possible and obtained which does not consist simply of civil servants being more pleasant to the people they are dealing with – a poor vision of administrative change, reduced to the modification of individual behaviours in face-to-face contact with users. To return to the example of the tax administrations, it is not in giving the short-term satisfaction of not paying what is owed that they will become more efficient from the taxpayer's point of view; it is when their methods of functioning, during collection of the tax, no longer increase the amount of this tax. However, the differences which exist in this area, ranging from 1 for the most efficient or most 'virtuous' countries – such as Sweden or the United States – to 3 for the bottom of the class – France, for example – show the progress that still remains to be achieved in the functioning of administrative organisations.

8 Conclusion

Putting forward a theory and a methodology for steering change in organisations cannot be concluded without tackling the question of their link with the cultural context in which they have been drawn up. Are they closely linked to this context – in this case, that of developed countries in the Western world – and consequently relatively unadaptable and inoperative in very different surroundings? This question is based on the fact that, no doubt due to the globalisation that characterises the world at the start of the twenty-first century, executives and managers like tackling such 'cultural' issues, sometimes according them an inordinate level of importance. There is no merger or acquisition which is not preceded by a harrowing interrogation on the 'compatibility of cultures', a subject on which there is no hesitation in initiating in-depth research. All business schools have, in their international management programmes, courses that are devoted to such questions and each one proposes, in its continuing education programmes, seminars for familiarising participants with the need to take action in very differentiated environments.

What is at cause here is the well-known 'human factor' which, as already pointed out, most organisations consider to be a problem, in the primary sense of the term.

TWO VISIONS OF CULTURE WHICH DO NOT HAVE THE SAME CONSEQUENCES IN TERMS OF CHANGE

Not only is this fascination understandable, at a moment when few companies can permit themselves the luxury of staying only on their domestic market and are launching themselves, sometimes at high speed, into internationalising their operations, but also some countries are using it to protect themselves from an over-rapid invasion of foreign operators or to justify the existence, in such countries, of practices that would not be acceptable elsewhere. From this point of view, the opacity of the system built up in Japan by the producers, distributors, public authorities and consumer associations and which has nothing in common with the commercial legislation in effect in this country, has long discouraged a high number of Western-world firms, from America in particular. This has enormously helped what is commonly called the 'Japanese miracle'. Similarly, today, the importance that the Chinese confer on relationships, or *guanxhi*, also leads many operators to favour 'joint ventures' when entering this market, to the detriment of creating full-ownership subsidiaries.

Nevertheless, it must be emphasised that, behind this passing craze, there are two definitions of culture that do not have the same consequences on the subject under discussion. The first is general and focuses on a few major lines that characterise the living habits in the countries under consideration and, more particularly, the manner of grasping interpersonal relationships. We might say that this represents the *container* culture, which every visitor perceives at the outset and that a few specialists in management have absolutely insisted on theorising. The word 'container' refers here to the superficial aspect of this part of culture. It means that one perceives that which surrounds, that which may possibly attract or disturb. It indicates that one glimpses that part of the iceberg that is above the sea, which is striking because we are not used to icebergs, but which dissimulates beneath the water the full amplitude of the phenomenon. Thus one might explain that some of the difficulties experienced at EuroDisney when it first opened were due to the Americans refusing to allow alcohol to be served in the restaurants with an emphasis on family values, even though the host country was celebrated above all for its wines; in the same way, one might say that the first Japanese industrials who established themselves in the United States had not understood the very special nature of labour relations in that country. Even if this is not a question of denying the extent of differences, or their occasional importance in the management of international operations, it is not an exaggeration to say that, in day-to-day management, a whole series of *romantic stereotypes* have been developed that have little to do with the action.

This is why we need to reach a second dimension of culture which is more practical, and above all more operative once it is a question of steering organisations in general and introducing change in particular. You will remember for this that we have defined an organisation as a set of actor strategies, as opposed to a definition based on organisation charts, rules or procedures.[1] When such strategies, which are in fact behaviours, solutions found by the actors to solve the problems which present themselves, appear repetitively, we might say that they constitute the organisation's culture. A rougher, although more illustrative, way of stating the same idea would be to say that culture is what *everybody must do in a human population in order to be accepted and survive in that population*. This is not the set of actor strategies, which would lead to a tautological vision assimilating organisation and culture, but the redundant strategies that the actors use when faced with the key questions that collective life asks of them. Thus, under this heading, one will put *a decision process*.

The best example would be of this cosmetics company, undisputed world leader in its market, which, at least in its marketing and commercial spheres, has for many years cultivated 'fuzzy' and divided responsibilities, even going so far as to forbid any organisation chart or definition of function. A decision – such as a product launch, for example – could only result from the *confrontation* of viewpoints; that is, interest, with market knowledge as the principal resource to be mobilised in winning the day. The result was a situation in which nobody could take advantage of the slightest monopoly and everybody depended on others to undertake any action. The environment created in this way was characterised by its hardness – offering not the slightest intra-organisational protection – and by the need for restrictive performance appraisal systems as well as conciliation boards before which actors had only small interest in presenting themselves in order to settle their disputes. Such a decision process is as far as it can be from that identified in the transport company, where it was primarily a question of being able to present, to higher levels of the hierarchy, a well reasoned *dossier* which guaranteed to whoever had drawn it up that they were *covered* in the event of a problem. We might call what we have just described as the *'content'* culture.

Here, the word 'content' indicates that we are close to the essential, to what is most important, to what is necessary to grasp before launching oneself into action. The container is the fruit's outer husk, the content is the fruit itself. Moving from the first to the second presupposes that one is no longer fascinated by the form, the beauty, the originality of appearance, that one agrees to remove the outer protection in order to reach the inner flesh. We rediscover the theme of investment in knowledge, which we have used as one of the major orientations for leading change. But it is also the distinction between symptoms and problems which returns to mind. The container culture is the one that remains at the level of the symptom, the sign, the warning, the 'misunderstood information'. The content culture stems from the problem; that is, the real mechanisms which are at work. It is indeed this that must be the subject of all attentions, at least in terms of management.

THE CONSEQUENCES OF THE DISTINCTION BETWEEN THE CONTAINER CULTURE AND THE CONTENT CULTURE

These two visions lead to a better understanding of why, in most cases, we overestimate the importance and concrete impact of cultural phenomena. In the case of the container culture, the tree hides the forest and the capacity for action generally finds itself penalised. Fascinated by *attitudes*, we tend to see only them, to find in them a root system together with a thousand years of history, and to think that their reappraisal is an impossible exploit.

This was how it was in the myth of life employment in Japan, which has resulted in the elaboration of sophisticated theories on the constraints of human resource management in Japan, although this was a recent phenomenon, linked to the present economic climate, that the Japanese themselves did not hesitate to question at the end of the 1980s, when difficult economic circumstances justified it.[2] In 2000, the senior executive sent by Renault to Nissan in order to save the company from bankruptcy, had no hesitation in reappraising the family-like links which, apparently, united the company and its most favoured suppliers, and drastically reducing the number, without this appearing to pose major problems but, what is more, doing the greatest good to the companies.[3]

This simple idea that, at least in terms of management, necessity to a great extent makes its own rules, is the basis for what we have called the content culture and is going to open interesting perspectives in terms of leading change and the transferability of methodologies and approaches, even if nobody will dispute all the nuances and cautions needed. This in fact implies that actors placed in a similar context are going to have, on *content*, roughly the same reactions, are going to find the same solutions, develop strategies that are close to each other in order to face up to identical managerial situations, while the *form* that such reactions will take can, in appearance, be very varied and, at first sight, exotic and surprising. An example will help to illustrate this proposal.

DIFFERENCES IN ATTITUDES AND COMMUNITIES OF STRATEGY

In the 1980s, we had the opportunity to carry out an in-depth survey on 'white' goods,[4] in the United States, Japan and France.[5] The purpose of this work was to understand, from a sociological point of view, the way in which the different operators making up a market – producers, distributors, consumers and their associations, public authorities – managed their relationships. Starting from this analysis, it became possible to understand the strength of the Japanese producers and the weakness of their French counterparts, not in terms of how the industrial apparatus functioned, an interpretation that was very popular at the time, but based on an understanding of the strategies developed by these different actors and of the relationships of power and dependency that held them together. This survey was carried out in an empirical fashion, on the basis of interviews conducted in the three countries, with the main parties concerned. Among the questions asked during these interviews, there was one that showed itself to be particularly fruitful and revealing in terms of the day-to-day reality of the so-called 'differences of culture'. This was addressed to producers of household electrical equipment and consisted of asking them, based on a situation that was painful to them, particularly in France, what their reactions were when a distributor took over one of their best known brands or products, and 'broke' the price in a logic of sales drift or shelf drift.[6]

The French replies were always embarrassed, hesitant and blamed the legislation in force at the time (prohibiting refusal to sell) which placed them in a situation of extreme dependency with regard to distributors, to whom they were not allowed to refuse their products. They therefore appealed to the good sense of public authority to re-establish a healthy balance between the players. Nevertheless, when driven into a corner, they finally admitted that they did have some possibilities of retaliation, even if very unofficial and consisting of either refusing to deliver the goods with a total disregard for regulations, or, when they had been trapped into it, buying back, themselves and in bulk, the stock of products purchased by the distributor, or, even more brutally, making available to the distributor a batch that had been 'inadvertently' damaged during transportation.

The same question addressed to an American provoked outright hilarity faced with a situation which he said he knew well, describing it humorously as 'Mickey Mouse business'. He did not need much time nor many pointless oratorical precautions to explain that, once such a distributor had been identified, he was subjected to an immediate and strict boycott, and that if, by mistake, delivery had been made, the products were bought back on opening, which did not prevent the culprit sometimes being sanctioned by surreptitiously procuring damaged equipment for him.

The Japanese showed themselves right away to be extremely shocked by the question, emphasising its brutal character, finally very 'Western', and putting the interpreter into an uncomfortable situation in which he vigorously manifested his agreement with the interviewee's reaction. The latter, with ostensibly reproachful patience, was explaining that this type of behaviour was impossible in Japan, where producers and distributors were connected with close links built up over time, and certainly did not have the same intensity or quality with his speakers for the day. And anyway, they added, if that did happen, there was a 'committee of honest trading' which supervised the legality and good faith of transactions. This affirmation was manifestly intended to put an end to the interview. But this had been carefully prepared and we had a few examples in mind which showed that similar

cases could have occurred. At the end of a good two hours of very disagreeable discussion, during which we had the feeling of adding, every
moment, to our impoliteness and boorishness, it was admitted, without
really spelling things out, that such a situation could have existed in times
and places that nobody could remember clearly. Looking back, somebody
remembered that, faced with this problem, one of the producers (but which
one?) had refused to deliver, eventually bought back the incriminated
stock and even took retaliatory measures, which we were led to understand
were the same as those mentioned in the two previous countries.

And so we find a new illustration of the distinction between the *container culture* and the *content culture*. Each of the speakers reacted to the
question asked in a totally different way and replied to it with an openness
or goodwill that revealed a wide diversity, if not total opposition, in the
management of inter-individual relationships. Evidently, the social codes
defining what can be said and what cannot, and determining the fashion of
conducting an interview (the possibility for the interviewer to insist when
he considers that the speaker has not answered the question), had little in
common with each other. Even the goal pursued by means of the answer
was not the same: the Frenchman disclaimed his responsibility and passed
on a message to the public authorities, the American immediately dis-
charged what he considered to be a naïvety, while the Japanese preferred
to maintain good relations with his usual long-term partners.

But apart from that, the *practices* which ended up being revealed, what
throughout this book we have referred to as strategies, were more or less
the same, expressing concrete methods of adaptation that were to all
intents and purposes identical. This observation made no inference on the
mechanisms of differentiation which were far deeper and could affect
social life in general, family or friends, the processes of integration or
rejection. It simply indicates that, in daily working life, there are proximi-
ties which are certainly stronger than one thinks, especially when one
allows oneself to be impressed by methods of expression, languages used,
including body language, which can be observed during a conversation of
the type that has been mentioned. But the management of organisations, is
not a form of tourism.

THE UNIVERSALITY OF THE THEORY
OF BOUNDED RATIONALITY

It is essential to draw all the consequences in terms of steering change.
One of the guiding ideas in this book is to show that, since actors are

intelligent – in the sociological sense of the term – there is no point in trying to convince them to act differently than they are doing, as long as one maintains them in an identical context. It is better to act on the levers to make their behaviour change and hence change the organisation. *This seems to be able to be applied in contexts that are very different at first sight.* In fact, the concept of levers covers a *mechanism*, this infers nothing on the *nature* of the lever used which, itself, is no doubt susceptible to major adaptations, in line with what are the most important issues for the actors.

In this way, at the time of a survey carried out at Wuhan in central China and focusing on the management of a 'joint venture' between an American company and the Chinese Ministry of Mail and Telecommunications, we were asking an expatriate in charge of managing this unit, about the reward system that he used to differentiate local managers and valorise their performances. He replied seriously that the length of the siesta was the most appropriate mechanism, to the extent that, for financial reasons, most of the managers in question carried out a second job during the night-time and that, because of this, the possibility of recovering slightly during the day was crucial! Nobody disputed the need to use a *lever*, but emphasis was placed on the necessity to find one that was suited to local reality, which only a good integration in the environment would no doubt make it possible to understand.

This is why, although remaining cautious, one can consider that what, in previous chapters, has been called the problematic and the methodology of change are largely transferable into contexts perceived in principle as very dissimilar. In fact, in the same way that the strategic analysis of organisations and systems in particular, and the theory of *bounded rationality* in general, does not in any way prejudice the substance of the subject being studied, the theory of change which is deduced from it, and which has been talked about in this book, is only marginally influenced by what are habitually called cultural contexts. This time, these relate more to the container than to the content.

ADAPTING THE STRATEGY

Yet one cannot say the same for what relates to the *strategy for change*, precisely because it is itself a container. We have already seen that this is the subject of discussions between the specialists on the precise point of knowing whether it is necessary to associate all the actors with the process or if, to the contrary, it is necessary to act quickly and strongly, creating a shock, without worrying too much about human considerations.[7]

All the restructuring, downsizing and other practices of the 1980s and 1990s have taught us that not all countries had the same capacity to survive their brutal and devastating effects. Some writers even think this capacity to be an important success factor in the competition for adaptation of economies and companies to the new realties.[8]

For ourselves, we have seen that the difficulty in consenting to instant sacrifices, renouncing advantages, or *protections* as we have said, severely compromises the possibility of operating the necessary transformations of the public sector in a country such as France, where the reform of the administration is continually put off until tomorrow, in other words, until the next government. The temptation is therefore great to use, not participative strategies such as those for which we have pleaded, but more radical actions in which the parties concerned submit or resign.

We continue to believe that the remedy would be worse than the ill, in the same way that we do not dispute the fact that the Americans would be wrong to ask questions that those who suffer the brutal changes imposed on them do not ask themselves. As in the proverb: 'When in Rome, do as the Romans do'.

Notes

Introduction

1. Beer, M., Eisensat, R. A. and Spector, B. (1990) 'Why change programs don't produce change', *Harvard Business Review*, November–December.
2. Kotter, J. P. (1995) 'Leading change: Why Transformation Efforts Fail', *Harvard Business Review*, March–April.
3. Drucker, P. F. (1999) *'Management Challenges for the 21st Century'*, Harper Business.
4. *Ibid.*
5. This is a recurrent theme in organisational sociology, which has been developed in France by Michel Crozier. See in particular: *La société bloquée* Editions du Seuil (1971). This theme is today once again up with the times; due to the extreme difficulty in getting public bodies to evolve: cf. Chapter 7.
6. We will return in more detail on this particular case at the end of this book.
7. We should – among others – add Chris Argyris (1993) *Knowledge for action: a guide to overcoming barriers to organizational change*, Jossey-Bass Management.
8. Argyris, C. (1991) 'Teaching smart people how to learn. Every company faces a learning dilemma: The smartest people find it the hardest to learn', *Harvard Business Review*, May–June, pp. 99–109.
9. Dupuy, F. (1998) *The Customer's Victory*, Macmillan Press Ltd – now Palgrave.
10. Reich, R. B. (1992) *The Work of Nations*, Vintage Books.
11. *The Customer's Victory, op. cit.*
12. In the meaning given to this expression by Herbert Simon. See March, J. G. and Simon, H A. (1958) *Organizations*, J. Wiley.
13. The expression comes from Peter Drucker.
14. This point will be discussed in more detail in the Conclusion.

1 Change: Yes, But What?

1. This vision is somewhat generalised and optimistic. It will be discussed and enlarged upon throughout this book.
2. Stermin, J. and Choo, R. (2000) 'The Power of Positive Deviancy', *Harvard Business Review*, January–February, pp. 14–15.
3. When we teach in business schools, it frequently happens that we are called upon to pronounce ourselves in favour of one 'system' or another for the reason that it really is necessary to make choices.
4. In the sociological meaning of 'control over what is important for other actors or for the organisation itself'.
5. We can refer you – although this is only one example from many – to Waterman *et al.* (1980): 'Structure is not organization', *Business Horizons*, vol. 23, no. 3, June 1980.

6.   Dupuy, F. and Thoenig, J.-C. (1985) *L'administration en miettes*, Fayard.
7.   This discussion will be continued in the second part of Chapter 6, focusing on implementation.
8.   We will return to this topic in Chapter 6 when analysing the Air France case study.
9.   Hammer, M. and Stanton, S. (1999) 'How process enterprises really work', *Harvard Business Review*, November–December, pp. 108–18.
10. The concept is borrowed from Sull, D. N. (1999) 'Why good companies go bad', *Harvard Business Review*, July–August, pp. 42–52.
11. There is much written on the difference between behaviours and attitudes. This is far more scientific than managerial, showing the progress that organisational management has yet to achieve. See: Crozier, M. and Friedberg, E. (1977) *L'acteur et le système*, Paris, Editions du Seuil.
12. Georges Moinaux Courteline, 1858/60?–1929. French writer and playwright celebrated for his humorous parody of French administration.
13. This is the case in particular of public organisations, for which this can sometimes be the start of a true revolution, cf. Chapter 7.
14. This complexity is outlined and analysed in Chapter 2.
15. In fact, they only occupy the space that they are allowed to take, or rather that the mechanisms of lack of knowledge leave them.
16. For the theoretical presentation, we refer you to Crozier and Friedberg, *op. cit*. For practical applications, we refer you to Dupuy, *The Customer's Victory, op. cit*, in particular chapter 6, 'The frame of reference'.
17. Cf. Chapter 5.

2   The Process: From Symptoms to Problems

1.   'The next frontier: Edgard Schein on organizational therapy', *The Academy of Management Executive*. vol. 14, no. 1, February 2000, pp. 31–48. It will be very interesting to read the commentary on this article written by Manfred Kets de Vries in the same issue.
2.   'Citygroup's John Reed and Standford's James March on management research and practice'. *The Academy of Management Executive*, vol. 14, no. 1, February 2000, pp. 52–64.
3.   Argyris, C., *Knowledge for action: a guide to overcoming barriers to organizational change.*
4.   See note 1.
5.   Sahti, R. K. and Beyerlein, M. M. (2000) 'Knowledge transfer and management consulting: a look at "the Firm"', *Business Horizons*, vol. 43, no. 1, January–February, pp. 65–74.
6.   Crozier, M. and Thoenig, J.-C. (1976) 'L'importance du système politico-administratif territorial', in Peyrefitte, A. *et al. Décentraliser les responsabilités. Pourquoi? Comment?*, Paris, la Documentation Française, pp. 55–106.
7.   The buyers were appraised on the unit cost of the products bought. They therefore had an interest in common with the suppliers, while the production manager had to keep a proper balance between this unit cost and the cost of the stock.
8.   This grid was presented in detail in *The Customer's Victory, op. cit.*

9. Cf. Chapter 1.
10. The 'industrial monopoly' has already been the subject of study during the 1960s by Michel Crozier. It subsequently became one of the most classic cases in organisational sociology. We have had the opportunity of studying this same company at the start of the 1990s just before it was privatised. It is on this second survey that we have based our argument, although the continuity of situations, 30 years on, is amazing. See Crozier, M. (1964) *The Bureaucratic Phenomenon*, University of Chicago Press.

3 The Process: Looking for the Priorities

1. See among others the example on change in a car company given by: Roth, G. and Kleiner, A. (2000) 'Car launch: The human side of managing change,' in Roth, G. and Kleiner, A. (eds), *The learning history library*, New–York, Oxford University Press.
2. Cf. the discussion at the end of Chapter 6.
3. This case has already been presented in another form in '*The Customer's Victory, op. cit.*
4. This is what one might call a 'paradoxical cooperation': people help each other to avoid the involvement of third parties, but never for the advantage of the organisation in its entirety.
5. Here, we can understand the vanity of the 'common sense speech' in these organisations. Explaining to account executives that they should communicate their information and that it is vital for the survival of the bank of which they are part, that is common sense. And yet, in an identical context, this has no sense for them, to the extent that it would result in giving up their principal resource.
6. This observation is not new. It has already been shown by Beer *et al.* in: 'Why change programs don't produce change', *op. cit.*
7. Public action mostly obeys this principle, dedicated by the official definition of what characterises the State: the monopoly of legitimate violence. One cannot say this better.
8. See Dupuy, F. and Thoenig, J.-C. (1979) 'Public transportation policy making in France as an implementation problem', *Policy Sciences*, vol. 11, pp. 1–18. Also by the same authors, *l'Administration en miettes, op. cit.*

4 The Process: From Priorities to Levers

1. The Taylorist concept of the universal rule which, because it ensures a system that is optimal, fair, legitimate, in relation to the goals to be achieved, would be imposed on all without discussion, is still very much alive. In recent times, this has been rediscovered in job descriptions, of course, but also in quality certifications. These have had to undergo profound changes in their philosophy, integrating the strategic dimension of human behaviour.
2. In Chapter 5, we will have the opportunity to return to problems of implementation which are more difficult to deal with in other ways than the definition of programmes and strategies.

3. Like culture, values only take on meaning in action, through concrete acts by actors. They then show themselves to be far more homogenous than they appeared to start with.
4   On the subject of project management, its advantages and its difficulties, we can refer to 'Où en est la gestion de projet?', *Le journal de l'Ecole de Paris*, no. 1, January 1997, pp. 17–26.
5. On the importance of managing human resources when conducting change, one can read: Ulrich, D. (1998) 'A new mandate for Human Resources', *Harvard Business Review*, January–February, pp. 125–34; also Begley, T. M. and Boyd, D. P. (2000) 'Articulating corporate values through Human Resource policy', *Business Horizon*, vol. 43, no. 4, July–August.
6. This is the case in the transport company – as soon as a delay is seen, a code is attributed to it, indicating clearly which team is involved in this delay. But allocating this code does not incur any consequence for that team. It is therefore not a lever and the person who controls it gains no power from it.
7. Drucker, P. *Management Challenges for the 21st Century*, *op. cit.*

5   Implementation: The Moment of Change

1. Noble, C. H. (1994) '*Building the strategy implementation network*', *Business Horizons*, vol. 42, no. 6, November–December, pp. 19–28.
2. In such circumstances, companies adopt a logic of action which is close to that of politics: it is programmatic; that is, turned towards the intentions, towards what must be achieved, the desirable, but takes little interest in implementation. However, everything shows that, in the political domain as in management, the main difficulty does not lie in drawing up programmes, but in their effective implementation.
3. Sull, D. N. 'Why good companies go bad', *op. cit.*
4. Hammer, M. and Stanton S., 'How process enterprises really work', *op. cit.*
5. Source: Daniels, J. and Radebaugh, L. H. (2001) '*International Business*', Prentice Hall, Upper Saddle River, New Jersey, 9th edition, p. 759.
6. A survey conducted in 1999 by the General Inspectorate of this Ministry established that not one of the actors in the survey had protested: tax collection in France is carried out at a cost which is sometimes three times higher than that observed in comparable countries such as Spain or the United States. The complexity of the tax system is not enough to explain this differential. It is indeed the methods of functioning and therefore the organisation which are at cause.
7. On the function of work protection and its reappraisal under the effects of globalisation and new economic logics, see: Castel, R. (1995) *Les métamorphoses de la question sociale, une chronique du salariat*, Paris, Fayard, collection 'L'espace du politique'.
8. See Dupuy, F. *The Customer's Victory*, *op. cit.*
9. See Chapter 7 devoted to the specific case of public organisations, which correspond best to this definition.
10. This issue will be discussed at length in Chapter 6.

11. Dominique Thomas has given a perfect analysis of the phenomenon in: 'Les employés d'assurance face au changement'. PhD dissertation for postgraduate degree in sociology at the Paris Institute of Political Studies, 1979.
12. Nigel Nicholson (1998) 'How hardwired is human behavior', *Harvard Business Review*, July–August, pp. 135–47.

6 Implementation: Playing on Trust

1. This is the name used for average revenue earned on the sale of a seat. When an airline is in difficulty, it tends to leave tour operators free to offer its seats at whatever price they want in order to be sure of filling the aircraft. In this way, it gradually loses control over its pricing policy and, finally, its turnover.
2. There appears to be a lot to say on the need, in this type of listening operation, to use interviewers who have been well trained and well prepared. This means collaborators who know the sociological usage that will be made of the material they are collecting and who, in particular, understand that the problem is not knowing whether or not the person replying to the question is telling the truth, but understanding what he is saying something interesting because he is the one saying it, from where he is in the organisation. This is the condition for developing the empathy necessary for the creation of an atmosphere of trust, which will provide the interview with its best input. This is something that cannot be improvised.
3. There were at the time 14 union organisations in the company, representing both central labour bodies and an impressive number of sectional unions.
4. This is an approach which was greatly inspired by the example of British Airways where it has been quickly forgotten that a few years ago the situation here was hardly more brilliant than that at Air France. The highlighting of the concept of 'seamless travelling' and its interpretation into the organisation's day-to-day methods of functioning were, together with drastic cost reductions, one of the main factors for this company's success. The problems that it lived through later do not in any way contradict the very positive lessons that can be drawn from this experience.
5. This penchant for abstraction commences very early, right from the start of training for managers in general and senior executives in particular, even in the best business schools where the fear of taking risks leads to making students and managers work on theoretical and stereotyped situations, on stylised case studies which will only be encountered extremely rarely in reality. It is very satisfying to see that once one accepts a little more uncertainty in the teaching process by making participants reflect on real-life situations – their own, in fact – they begin to take real pleasure in this. They discover that reality is not a threat, that one can talk about it, discuss it, provided one has the right tools to bring it to light.
6. In 'The next frontier: Edgard Schein on organizational therapy', *op. cit.*, p. 38.
7. Manzoni, J.-F. and Barsoux, J.-L. (1998) 'The set-up-to-fail syndrome', *Harvard Business Review*, March–April, pp. 101–13.
8. These have been presented and developed by Michael Beer and Nitin Nohria in: 'Cracking the code of change', *Harvard Business Review*, May–June 2000, pp. 133–41. We summarise here the main points of their statement, even if we

do not necessarily share their optimism when it concerns the possibility of combining the two approaches.

9.   Cf. Chapter 7 on the specific case of public organisations.
10.   Cf. *The Customer's Victory, op. cit.*

7   The Particular Case of Public Organisations

1.   This chapter repeats a communication made at the OECD symposium 'Government of the future, from here to there', held in Paris on 14 and 15 September 1999. This communication was called 'Why is it so difficult to reform public organizations?'.
2.   In *'The Customer's Victory'*, *op. cit.*
3.   Castel, R., *op. cit.*
4.   See Rifkin, J. (1996) 'The end of the work: the decline in the global labour force with the dawn of the lost modern era.' Paris, la Découverte, 2000 and Reich, R. (1993) 'The work of Nations: preparing ourselves for the 21st century capitalism.' Vintage books, 1992.
5.   Duran, P. (1999) *Penser l'action publique*, Paris, LGDJ.
6.   See, for example: Garcia, A. (2000) 'La "crise des vocations" accentue le malaise des hauts fonctionnaires', *Le Monde*, 2 November.
7.   This was the case during the famous 'strikes by proxy' at the end of 1995 in France against the reforms proposed by the Juppé government.
8.   French national employment office.
9.   This is the case in Ireland, Sweden, New Zealand and the Netherlands.
10.   Cf. Chapter 2.
11.   We have already mentioned in Chapter 5 the probability that the main obstacle in France to the merger between the General Tax Division and Public Accounting is the sharing out of these two entities between Syndicat Unifié des Impôts on one side, and Force Ouvrière on the other.
12.   It is here that the word 'culture' takes on all its practical meaning. If one uses it to designate, not just a few abstract norms, but routine ways of dealing with questions which return most frequently on the agenda, then the administrative culture is very strong. Often, this starts to be learned in family life, then continues to be developed within the educational establishments attended. Its adoption, in this context more so than anywhere else, is necessary for a good integration in the environment, and therefore for a successful career in it. Here there is a number of areas in which one does not succeed against the system, but with it; that is with others.

8   Conclusion

1.   Cf. Chapter 1.
2.   See, for example, Koshiro, K. (1984) 'Life employment in Japan', *Monthly Labour Review*, August; or Tsurumi, Y. (1993) 'Executive Commentary', *Academy of Management Executive*, vol. 7, no. 4.
3.   'Sous la houlette de Renault, Nissan renoue avec les profits', *Le Monde*, 30 October 2000.

4. This is what one calls electrical appliances for the kitchen (cooker, microwave, dishwasher, and so on) as opposed to 'brown' goods, for the living room (television, hi-fi, and so on).
5. Dupuy, F. and Choenig, J.-C. (1986) *La Loi du Marché. L'électroménager en France aux Etats-Unis et au Japon*, Collection Logiques Sociales, Paris, L'Harmattan.
6. Current practice, especially in France.
7. Cf. Chapter 6.
8. This is the case of Robert Waterman in *What America Does Right*, Plume-Penguin, New York, 1995.

Glossary

Note: The definitions given in this glossary are not academic in nature. They make reference to what has been developed in this book and are intended to facilitate reading. For teaching purposes we have preferred to keep to simple and practical definitions.

Actor(s): The actor can be individual or collective; it is defined by its *relevance* in relation to the organisation being studied; that is by the necessity to take it into consideration in order to understand the reality of this organisation. The overall set of stable relationships between relevant actors forms a system.

Analysis grid: One of two tools in the strategic analysis of organisations. Makes it possible in a simple format to make links between the context, the problems to be resolved and the strategies of actors. Is only useful when accompanied by excellent understanding of the conceptual context underpinning it.

Arrangement(s): Solution(s) found by actors through the confrontation of their divergent interests. All arrangements have a cost, not only financial. It is easier for actors to find an arrangement where they externalise the cost onto third parties.

Attitudes: The most apparent way in which an actor reacts or expresses itself. Assumed to depend on the actor itself and its intention, attitudes are understood in opposition to behaviours which are themselves of a contextual nature. The distinction between the two is the subject of endless debates between sociologists.

Autonomy: Situation in which an actor succeeds in avoiding any situation of dependence on others. The search for autonomy appears empirically to be the most widely found problem in organisations.

Bureaucracy: Organisation which is characterised by the endogenous nature of all the criteria that it uses and which builds its methods of functioning on its own constraints and not on those of its relevant environment. In managerial language, in contrast with customer-organisation.

Change: Substantial and durable modification from the strategies of actors, such as these are expressed in their daily behaviour. In contrast with the modification of structures.

Concrete: Close to 'reality'. Designates what exists effectively, as opposed to what should exist. Taking it into account is one of the conditions for a successful action of change. Methods of functioning are concrete, structures are not.

Confidence: Acknowledgment of the capacity of actors to accept reality such as it is. Involvement of such actors in looking for solutions.

Context: The actor's relevant environment, made up of a set of resources and constraints, including rules, procedures or other actors.

138

The actor's intelligence allows it to adapt by seeking to obtain what can be obtained in the context such as it is. It is the change of context which allows change in the strategy of actors, therefore in the organisation.

Constraints: One of the elements in the context of actors: what they must face up to in order to resolve their problems. Can be material elements or other actors. Are never fixed once and for all. In contrast with resources.

Cooperation: Designates the direct confrontation of the diverging interests of actors and the immediate search for a negotiated solution acceptable to them. Is neither natural nor spontaneous since it reduces autonomy. Must therefore be constructed with the help of levers. Involves simultaneity and thus makes it possible to reduce costs and lead-times. In contrast with coordination.

Coordination: Both an activity and a function. Consists of getting a third party actor to manage the logics, timings, decisions and the actions of actors who are not cooperating. The multiplication of coordination functions is one of the characteristics of bureaucratic organisations.

Culture (company): Package of strategies which are found recurrently in an organisation. Predominant way in which actors in this organisation resolve their problems.
'Containing' culture: Appearance, speech, external signals;
'Contained' culture: Concrete practices, strategies.

Dependence: Situation in which an actor sees another actor controlling something of importance for it. In contrast with autonomy.
Inversed dependence: situation in which real dependence is in contrast with hierarchical. Characteristic of bureaucratic organisations.

Empowerment: Action of giving actors the intellectual and methodological means allowing them to go beyond their partial view of reality. Giving the means of knowledge and not just the knowledge itself.

Implementation: Device adopted in order to bring envisaged solutions into effect. Concerns both the conditions of associating actors with the process and bringing overall management systems into concordance with what one wishes to obtain from these actors.

Intelligence: Capacity of any actor to find an acceptable solution for itself, in the context in which it exists. Basic postulate in the theory of bounded rationality.

Knowledge: Apprehension or organisational mechanisms which are at work and which characterise the system on which analysis is focusing. Is identified with the understanding of problems. Refers to reality and concreteness. Knowledge sharing: circulation of what has been updated to all actors concerned. Is identified with 'listening'. Involves confidence.

Levers: Component parts of the context of actors on which one can play in order to achieve progress in their problem-solving

Levers *cont.*	and strategies. The systems for managing human resources are the levers that are most frequently used. We talk of leverage effect.
Bounded rationality:	Calculation (conscious or unconscious) made by an actor in a given context in order to find a solution acceptable to it. In contrast with absolute rationality which presupposes the existence of a single good solution.
Listening:	Action consisting of putting feelings expressed by actors to the evidence of their reality, beyond the partial and partisan perception that they have of them. Listening is not asking actors what they want, it is saying it to them based on an understanding of their concrete working world.
Management:	Obtaining from actors for whom one is responsible that they do what one wants them to do.
Margin(s) for manoeuvre:	Area of freedom possessed by an actor allowing it to act on the context of other actors in order to cause them to change strategies. Often underestimated by the actors themselves. Can only be identified by knowledge.
Method:	Arrangement of the different phases of a process of change. Concerns the way of proceeding and not the content. In contrast with model.
Method of: reasoning	Set of notions and concepts arranged in relation to one another enabling an understanding of the reality. The strategic analysis of organisations and systems is a method of reasoning. In contrast with model.
Methods of functioning:	Expression used to differentiate between organisation and structure. Concrete and day-to-day way in which actors organise themselves to ensure the sustainability of the environment in which they are developing.
Methodological realism:	Postulate which means that an action (of change) can only be controlled and effective if it is based on a thorough knowledge of reality.
Monopoly:	Organisation where the dominant actors have a strong capacity to make their environment – which has no choice – bear the cost of their internal arrangements. Within an organisation, an overly precise definition of functions and territories leads to the formation of internal monopolies.
Opportunity(ies):	Designates here the fact for an actor to succeed in transforming a constraint into a resource, for itself or for another actor. The play of actors with their resources and constraints is known as management of opportunists.
Organisation:	Designates the overall strategies of actors, what they do, the way in which they work and resolve their problems. Must be differentiated from the structure which is only one of the elements in the context of such actors. Relates to concreteness and reality.
Outsourcing (of costs):	Organisational mechanism through which the actors in a system cause actors outside this system to bear the costs of arrangements that they have organised. The same

	mechanisms exist within organisations on behalf of actors who are dominant and/or in a situation of monopoly.
Play:	Stable arrangement of the strategies of relevant actors, leading to the permanence and stability of a system. Play with: use, employ.
Power:	An actor has power when it controls something important for another actor or for the organisation in general. Power is not an attribute. It only exists in the relationship with others. Different from hierarchy.
Priority(ies):	Part of a system, either a field, or a category, which an action of change will attack first, to the extent that it makes it possible to unbalance the system. Does not necessarily cover the most important problem. Is found at the junction of the desirable with the possible.
Problem(s):	Used here with two meanings: An information understood: meaning organisational mechanisms making it possible to interpret the symptoms which have drawn attention; Problem to be resolved: what an actor seeks to achieve in the context in which it finds itself. Different from task or assignment. Does not mean that the actor 'has a problem' in the usual sense of the term, but that it wishes to obtain something.
Protection (function of):	Expression used with regard to work in developed companies. Organisations have a natural tendency to develop this function to the detriment of that of production turned towards the environment. Market pressure inverses this tendency.
Reality:	Designates the concrete conditions in which actors find themselves and which explain why they do what they are doing. The starting point for initiating an action of change. In contrast with appearance and generally with structure, rules and procedures.
Resources:	One of the elements in the context of actors. What they can activate in order to resolve the problems that they are seeking to resolve. Can be material elements (rules and procedures) or other actors. Are never fixed once and for all. In contrast with constraints. Principal resource of the most powerful actor: the 'hard' point of an organisation. The point that must generally be attacked in order to obtain true change.
Site:	Part or activity of an organisation that has been identified as being sufficiently important to be the subject of special treatment, in the context of a project for change.
Sociogram:	One of two tools in the strategic analysis of organisations. Visualisation of relationships between actors, such as can be perceived by getting them to express their feelings about one another. Is built on a simple qualification: positive, negative or neutral. Must be considered as a dynamic tool which makes it possible to ask the questions that the analysis grid will help to elucidate.

Strategic analysis of organisations:	Method of reasoning (concepts) and tools (sociogram and analysis grid) that make it possible to apprehend organisations as a set of rational actor strategies. Strategic reasoning will be spoken of.
Strategy:	Acceptable solution – but not necessarily the best – found by an actor in a given context in order to achieve what it is seeking to achieve. Concrete expression of the actor's intelligence.

Rational strategy: in the meaning of bounded rationality (Herbert Simon). Does not mean either that the actor is right, or approved. In contrast with irrationality, stupidity, dishonesty which are not sociological concepts.

Symptom(s):	Term borrowed from medical language which designates what appears, what gives the alarm signal: defects, excessive delays, financial losses. It is a 'not understood information' that analysis will help to transform into an 'understood information', that is, into an identified problem.
System:	Overall strategies of actors only understood in relation to one another. A system presupposes a certain degree of stability. Sociology uses the phrase concrete action system to indicate that this is a reality which has meaning for the actors.
Uncertainty:	Important element for an actor, but which is not dependant on the actor. Whoever controls an uncertainty has power; whoever is subject to this control is in a situation of dependence. Conventional sociology talks of 'area of uncertainty' to express the idea that uncertainty is generally poorly defined.

Relevant uncertainty: refers to the idea that, in order to give power, the uncertainty being controlled must be significant for another actor or for the organisation itself.

Unexpected effects:	Result different from that expected or uncontrolled result of an action or a decision for change. Occur generally when investment in knowledge has not been adequate.

Bibliography

The Academy of Management Executive (2000) 'The next frontier: Edgard Schein on organizational therapy', *The Academy of Management Executive*, vol. 14, no. 1, February, pp. 31–48.

The Academy of Management Executive (2000) 'Citygroup's John Reed and Stanford's James March on management research and practice', *The Academy of Management Executive*, vol. 14, no. 1, February, pp. 52–64.

ARGYRIS, C. (1991) 'Teaching smart people how to learn. Every company faces a learning dilemma: the smartest people find it the hardest to learn', *Harvard Business Review*, May–June, pp. 99–109.

ARGYRIS, C. (1993) *Knowledge for action: a guide for overcoming barriers to organizational change,* Jossey-Bass Management.

BEER, M., EISENSAT, R. A. and SPECTOR, B. (1990) 'Why change programs don't produce change', *Harvard Business Review*, November–December.

BEER, M. and NOHRIA, N. (2000) 'Cracking the code of change', *Harvard Business Review*, May–June, pp. 133–41.

BEGLEY, T. M. and BOYD, D. P. (2000) 'Articulating corporate values through Human Resource policy', *Business Horizon*, vol. 43, no. 4, July–August.

CROZIER, M. (1964) *The Bureaucratic Phenomenon*, University of Chicago Press.

CROZIER, M. (1971) *La société bloquée*, Seuil.

CROZIER, M. and FRIEDBERG, E. (1990) *Actors and systems*, University of Chicago Press.

CROZIER, M. and THOENIG, J.-C. (1976) 'L'importance du système politico-administratif territorial', in Peyrefitte, A. *et al.*, *Décentraliser les responsabilités. Pourquoi? Comment?*, la Documentation Française, pp. 55–106.

DANIELS, J. D. and RADEBAIGHT, L. H. (2000) *International Business Environments and Operations*, Prentice Hall, 9th edn.

DRUCKER, P. F. (1999) *Management Challenges for the 21st Century*, Harper Business.

DUPUY, F. (1999) *The Customer's Victory*, Macmillan Press Ltd – now Palgrave.

DUPUY, F. (1999) 'Why is it so difficult to reform public organizations?', OECD Symposium 'Government of the Future, from here to there', Paris, 14–15 September.

DUPUY, F. and THOENIG, J.-C. (1979) 'Public transportation policy making in France as an implementation problem', *Policy Sciences*. vol. 11, pp. 1–18.

DUPUY, F. and THOENIG, J.-C. (1985) *L'administration en miettes*, Fayard.

DUPUY, F. and THOENIG, J.-C. (1986) *La Loi du Marché. L'électroménager en France aux Etats-Unis et au Japon*, Collection Logiques Sociales, L'Harmattan.

DURAN, P. (1999) *Penser l'action publique*, LGDJ.

GARCIA, A. (2000) 'La "crise des vocation" accentue le malaise des hauts fonctionnaires', *Le Monde*, 2 November.

HAMMER, M. and STANTON, S. (1999) 'How process enterprises really work', *Harvard Business Review*, November–December, pp. 108–18.

Le Journal de l'Ecole de Paris (1997) 'Où en est la gestion de Projet?', no. 1, January, pp. 17–26.

143

KOSHIRO, K. (1984) 'Life employment in Japan', *Monthly Labor Review*, August.

KOTTER, J. P. (1995) 'Leading change: why transformation efforts fail', *Harvard Business Review*, March–April.

MANZONI, J.-F. and BARSOUX, J.-L. (1998) 'The set-up-to-fail syndrome', *Harvard Business Review*, March–April, pp. 101–13.

MARCH, J. G. and SIMON, H. A. (1958) *'Organizations'*, J. Wiley.

NICHOLSON, N. (1998) 'How hardwired is human behavior', *Harvard Business Review*, July–August, pp. 135–47.

NOBLE, C. H. (1999) 'Building the strategy implementation network', *Business Horizons*, vol. 42, no. 6, November–December, pp. 19–28.

REICH, R. B. (1992) *The work of nations: preparing ourselves for the 21st century capitalism*, Vintage Books.

RIFKIN, J. (1996) *The end of work: the decline in the global labor force with the dawn of the post modern era*, la Découverte.

ROTH, G. and KLEINER, A. (2000) 'Car launch: the human side of managing change', in Roth, G. and Kleiner, A. (eds), *The learning history library*, Oxford University Press.

SAHTI, R. K. and BEYERLEIN, M. M. (2000) 'Knowledge transfer and management consulting: a look at "the Firm"', *Business Horizons*, vol. 43, no. 1, January–February, 65–74.

STERMIN, J. and CHOO, R. (2000) 'The Power of Positive Deviancy', *Harvard Business Review*, February, pp. 14–15.

SULL, D. N. (1999) 'Why good companies go bad', *Harvard Business Review*, July–August, pp. 42–52.

THOMAS, D. (1979) 'Les employés d'assurance face au changement', PhD dissertation, Paris Institute of Political Studies.

TSURUMI, Y. (1993) 'Executive commentary', *Academy of Management Executive*, vol. 7, no. 4.

ULRICH, D. (1998) 'A new mandate for Human Resources', *Harvard Business Review*, January–February, pp. 125–34.

WATERMAN, R. H. (1995) *What America Does Right*, Plume-Penguin.

WATERMAN, R. H., PETERS, T. J. and PHILLIPS, J. R. (1980) 'Structure is not Organization', *Business Horizons*, vol. 23, no. 3, June.

Index